OUR SOVEREIGN GOD

OUR SOVEREIGN GOD

Knowing and Serving the Lord of All

Edited by James Montgomery Boice

P.O. BOX 817 • PHILLIPSBURG • NEW JERSEY 08865-0817

Previously issued 2008 by Solid Ground Christian Books
Reissued 2023 by P&R Publishing

ISBN: 978-1-62995-862-0 (pbk)
ISBN: 978-1-62995-949-8 (ePub)

Printed in the United States of America

Library of Congress Cataloging-in-Publication Data has been applied for.

To him
who sitteth upon the throne,
and unto the Lamb

Contents

Editor's Preface

IT IS appropriate that the first book to appear as a result of the Philadelphia Conference on Reformed Theology should bear the title *Our Sovereign God.* The sovereignty of God has been an emphasis of the conference from the beginning, and it is a most vital theme.

The conference has three announced objectives. The first objective is "to awaken a new interest in biblical theology and to give greater visibility to the doctrines of grace through the church generally." Those involved in the planning and execution of the conference believe that there is a spiritual awakening in our time. However, that awakening is biblically and doctrinally shallow and comes at a time when the churches, for the most part, are ill-equipped to provide the necessary depth.

The second objective is "to establish a forum at which men and women in the Reformed tradition (from all denominations) might meet and be encouraged by others of like mind." This objective is linked to the first, for spiritual awakening is never simply a private affair, still less is it ever the work of a single individual.

Here the Puritans are a superb example. What made these men effective under God in so completely transforming both England and Scotland? There were many factors, of course. For one thing, these men were scholars, a fact which is often forgotten. They were steeped in the Word of God. They were diligent. No work was too great or mountain too high for them to tackle.

They were pious men who spent long hours in study and on their knees. They were not looking for promotions to positions of greater and greater prominence. Rather, they were willing to stay in one place, so the work of bringing the Word fully to that place might be completed. In addition, it must also be said that the Puritans knew one another, prayed for one another, assisted one another, loved one another. That is, they worked together in the great task of confronting their age with the gospel. Something of this spirit has also gripped many of those who have been attending the Philadelphia Conference annually.

The third objective of the conference is "to marshal resources to the end that believers might propagate the faith more effectively and thus 'establish, strengthen, and settle' the church upon the firm foundation of the doctrines of the apostles." The conference staff is anxious to see this objective realized. They pray that in the last quarter of the twentieth century the doctrines of God's sovereignty and grace might be sounded forth with new vigor, and that the God of grace might work through them to bring forth blessing and revival.

From the secular perspective, these are not at all great days. At the time of the first conference in Philadelphia in 1974, a religion reporter for one of the large daily newspapers called to ask about the conference. "Why should your conference amount to anything?" he asked. "People are disillusioned today, and many are apathetic. Many will not even know what the title of your conference or the phrase 'Reformed theology' means. Why should this venture be successful?" It was a fair question, but there was a good answer. First, many people are looking for answers in new places precisely *because* they are disillusioned. The rebirth of interest in the eastern religions is one symptom of their inner hunger. The Jesus movement is another. There is a striking interest in religious questions among young people, many of whom have since thronged the various conference meetings.

Second, because the doctrines of the Reformed faith are true, they have a unique ability to capture and enthrall the minds of men. When they are acknowledged to be true, they illuminate the mind and transform the individual perceiving them.

Finally, there is an undeniable connection between these doctrines and the periods of greatest advance for Christianity in the western world. Wherever one turns in church history, it is evident that the doctrines of grace have spawned religious awakenings. By the power of the Spirit of God, those doctrines have given birth to every spiritual renewal—from the sixteenth-century Reformation in Europe to the seventeenth-century revivals in England and Scotland to the eighteenth-century awakenings in England and America to the nineteenth-century recovery of true religion and godliness in England under Charles Haddon Spurgeon. Luther, Calvin, Zwingli, Knox, Baxter, Bunyan, Henry, Edwards, Whitefield, and Spurgeon (not to mention the host of confessors and martyrs who preceded them in church history) were all Calvinists. It was the fearless proclamation of the whole counsels of God, including the distinct doctrines of the Reformed faith, which God used to turn millions to Christ in those centuries.

Why should not the same be true in our day? May God use this volume, the conference of which it is a product, and other similar ventures as one part of a widespread spiritual renewal and revival so desperately needed in our time.

James Montgomery Boice

1

The Sovereignty of God the Son

JOHN R. W. STOTT

I IMAGINE that most of us are aware that the words "Jesus is Lord" constituted the very earliest Christian creed. If anybody in the early days confessed that Jesus Christ is Lord, he or she was accepted for baptism as a Christian believer. For it was recognized, on the one hand, that nobody can say that Jesus is Lord except by the Holy Spirit (1 Cor. 12:3), and, on the other hand, that if you confess with your lips that Jesus is Lord and believe in your heart that God has raised him from the dead, you will be saved (Rom. 10:9). In Greek the confession "Jesus is Lord" is only two words (*kurios Iesous*). It seems extraordinary that just two words could be a sufficient basis for the acceptance of a man or woman as a candidate for baptism. The reason is that these two words are pregnant with meaning. They signify both a theological conviction about Jesus Christ and a personal commitment to him.

What Does It Mean?

To say Jesus is Lord implies at least two things: (1) that Jesus is God and (2) that Jesus is Savior. In the Greek version of the Old Testament, the word *kurios* is used to translate the Hebrew word *Yahweh* or *Jehovah*. That is why in our English Bibles *Jehovah* is not translated as *Jehovah*. Instead, we have the word *LORD*. The writers of the New Testament knew that in the Old Testament *kurios* referred to God. But knowing this they did not hesitate to transfer the title to Jesus. That is tantamount to saying that Jesus is Jehovah.

They went further than that. They not only transferred to Jesus the title of God from the Old Testament. They also reapplied to Jesus verses in the Old Testament that alluded to Jehovah. One example is Isaiah 45:23. God himself is speaking, and he says, "I have sworn by myself . . . that unto me every knee shall bow, every tongue shall swear." Finding this in Isaiah, the apostle Paul with great audacity given him by the Holy Spirit transfers it to Jesus. Thus, he says in Philippians 2:9–11 that God has exalted Jesus and "given him a name which is above every name: that at the name of Jesus every knee should bow . . . and that every tongue should confess that Jesus Christ is Lord." So the New Testament authors did not hesitate to transfer to Jesus the title that was given to Jehovah and verses that applied to Jehovah in the Old Testament.

Not only so, but the New Testament authors did not feel a need to argue that Jesus is Jehovah. They argued justification by faith because it was being challenged in the church. But you do not find them arguing the deity of Jesus. Within a few years of the resurrection and ascension of Jesus, the assertion that Jesus Christ is Lord was already the universal faith of the Christian church. He is God, and he deserves worship. Jesus shares in the absolute supremacy of the Father and is worthy of the honor that is due to God alone.

To say Jesus is Lord also means that Jesus is Savior. It has been customary in some evangelical circles to distinguish rather sharply between Jesus the Savior and Jesus the Lord. It has been suggested that it is possible and even respectable to trust in Jesus as your Savior, yet not surrender to him as Lord. Such teaching is biblically indefensible. For not only is Jesus our Lord and Savior—he is the Lord Jesus Christ, the one and indivisible Christ—but his lordship implies his salvation and actually announces it.

So it is impossible to affirm Jesus as Lord without thereby affirming that Jesus is Savior. The title *Lord* is a symbol of Christ's victory over the forces of evil. If Jesus has been exalted over all the principalities and powers of evil, as indeed he has, this is the reason why he has been called Lord. If Jesus has been proclaimed Lord, as he has, it is because these powers are under his feet. He has conquered them on the cross, and therefore our salvation—that is to say, our rescue from sin, Satan, fear, and death—is due to that victory.

How then can we listen to the false accusations of our conscience if Satan, the slanderer, has been dethroned and disarmed by the Lord? If Jesus has conquered this slanderer, why do we listen to the false accusations of conscience? Of course, our conscience sometimes truly accuses us—I am not writing of that—but Satan often tries to get our consciences to accuse us falsely. Why listen if Jesus as the Lord has conquered him? Why do we remain in the bondage of evil if Jesus the Lord has broken its power?

Why should we be paralyzed by fear? Many Christians are paralyzed by fear: fear of the unknown, the occult, circumstances, people, demons, the number 13. How can we be paralyzed by fear if the very things of which we are afraid are under the feet of Jesus? Jesus is Lord. What are we afraid of? It is under his feet. How can we dread death? How can we think of death as anything but a trivial episode, a transit lounge between life here and life in its fullness, if Jesus the Lord has destroyed death and him who has the power of death, that is, the devil? It is because of the supreme lordship of Jesus over sin and death that we ourselves can be saved from death.

The apostle Peter understood this very well. So in the first Christian sermon, preached on the Day of Pentecost, Peter said, "You killed Jesus, but God has exalted him and has set him at his own right hand, and at that supreme place of honor and executive authority Jesus has received the Spirit from the Father and has shed forth this that you now see and hear" (see Acts 2:23, 33). In other words, Jesus has the authority to bestow on his church salvation, the forgiveness of sins, and the gift of the Spirit because he is Lord. Our salvation, our receiving of salvation, and our receiving of the gift of the Spirit are due to the fact that he is at the right hand of God. It is from that position that he saves us. That there is no salvation without lordship is the doctrine of the New Testament. Indeed, the two great affirmations "Jesus is Lord" and "Jesus saves" are virtually synonymous.

An Everlasting Title

Jesus is Lord. But where did he get that title? How did he come to win it for himself? There are three stages.

First, Jesus has possessed the title eternally because he is eternally God. For example, in 1 Corinthians 8:5–6 we read that, although there are many so-called gods and lords in the world today, yet for us Christians there is one God the Father, from whom are all things and for whom we exist, and one Lord Jesus Christ, through whom are all things and through whom we exist. The creed affirms that the Father is Lord, the Son is Lord, and the Spirit is Lord; yet there are not three Lords, but one. So the Father,

Son, and Holy Spirit together share in this eternal lordship that belongs to the persons of the Trinity as God. There has never been a time when Jesus, the second person of the Trinity, was not Lord.

Second, Jesus brought the title with him when he came to earth. When he became man, he did not cease to be God. When he became a servant, he did not cease to be the Lord. Have you ever thought how wonderful the angelic announcement of his nativity to the shepherds was? It was not, "Unto you is born this day in the city of David a Savior who is the Lord's Christ." That was not the announcement. Rather, by a subtle change from the genitive to the nominative it was "a Savior, who is Christ the Lord" (Luke 2:11). That is, he is himself the Lord; he is not merely the Lord's Anointed but the Anointed who *is* the Lord. He brought that title with him when he came to earth so that the unheard-of happened—the baby wrapped in swaddling clothes was declared by the angel to be our God and Savior.

During his public ministry, Jesus gave good evidence of his self-consciousness. He knew himself to be the Lord. He announced, for example, that with his coming into the world the kingdom of God had arrived. God's kingly rule had come. People could now receive and inherit it by being related to him. Moreover, in the upper room Jesus said to the apostles gathered around him, "You call me Master and Lord: and you say well; for so I am" (John 13:13). It is noteworthy that he said that just after he had gotten on his hands and knees to wash his disciples' feet. Just after he had visibly become their servant, he publicly proclaimed himself to be their Lord. Their Lord became their servant, and it is this combination of lordship and servitude that constitutes that paradox that is still the greatest evidence of the deity of Jesus. This is what we imply when we say that Jesus is Lord.

There is a third way in which Jesus has been given the title *Lord*. He was specifically accorded that title at his exaltation to the right hand of God. Jesus never predicted his sufferings without going on to predict his exaltation. He said that the Son of Man would be killed, but he added that on the third day he would rise again. The Son of Man must suffer but through his sufferings enter into glory. Jesus even dared to apply to himself the verse that reads: "The LORD said unto my Lord, Sit you at my right hand, until I make your enemies your footstool" (Ps. 110:1). Before the high priest, Jesus said, "You shall see the Son of man sitting on the right hand of [God]" (Mark 14:62).

So Jesus is Lord three times over: first, by right of his Godhead, sharing the throne of God; second, by right of his historical ministry, ushering in the kingdom of God; and third, by right of his supreme exaltation, sitting at the right hand of God. Jesus is three times Lord and thus deserves our full homage and our worship.

Practical Implications

This brings us to the crux of this chapter: the implications of Jesus's title. The Bible is not interested in doctrine without practice. Truth in Holy Scripture is always something not only to be known but to be acted upon. So the question before us is not only "Do we understand the doctrine that Jesus Christ is Lord?" but "What are the practical implications of that for us in our lives?" I want to suggest six major implications.

An Intellectual Implication

Jesus is Lord of our minds. I begin with our minds because the mind is the inner citadel that controls our actions. As we think, so we are.

I remind you of that beautiful invitation in which Jesus said, "Come unto me, all you who labor and are heavy laden, and I will give you rest. Take my yoke upon you, and learn of me; for I am meek and lowly in heart: and you shall find rest unto your souls" (Matt. 11:28–29). Christ's original hearers would have had no difficulty in understanding what he meant, because in those days everybody spoke of the yoke of Torah, the yoke of the Law of Moses. They regarded the Torah as a divine yoke that had been laid upon them by God himself. But knowing that, Jesus boldly set up his own teaching (in which he both endorsed the Law of Moses and transcended it) as a new yoke to which his disciples must submit.

Later he commissioned them to pass on to their converts everything that he had commanded them. Similarly, the apostle Paul writes of "casting down imaginations, and every high thing that exalts itself against the knowledge of God, and bringing into captivity every thought to the obedience of Christ" (2 Cor. 10:5). This is absolutely fundamental to biblical Christianity, because no man or woman is truly converted who is not intellectually converted. And nobody can claim to be intellectually converted who has not brought his or her mind into submission to the authority of Jesus as Lord.

Jesus is our teacher about God, man, duty, destiny, life, death, righteousness, Scripture, tradition—you name it. Jesus is our authority in each area, and the Christian is not at liberty to disagree with him. To disagree with Jesus, as Paul writes, is proud and arrogant (1 Tim. 6:4), and it is insubordinate (Titus 1:10–11). A false teacher, who disagrees with the teaching of Christ, is like an insubordinate adolescent. We must not be ashamed to say so in the church today. In the contemporary situation, where the wildest things are being taught by church leaders in the name of Jesus, it is urgent to recall the whole church to that humble position that properly belongs to it. It is to be under the teaching yoke of the Lord.

An Ethical Implication

Jesus is the Lord of our wills and of our moral standards. It is not only *what we believe* that is to come under the lordship of Jesus but also *how we behave*. Discipleship implies obedience, and obedience implies that there are absolute moral commands that we are required to obey. To refer to Jesus politely as "our Lord" is not enough. He still says to us, "Why do you call me Lord, Lord, and do not the things which I say?" (Luke 6:46). In today's miasma of relativity, we need to maintain unashamedly the absolute moral standards of the Lord. Further, we need to go on and teach that the yoke of Jesus is easy and his burden is light, and that under the yoke of Jesus we have not bondage but freedom and rest.

A Vocational Implication

Jesus is Lord of our careers, professions, jobs, ambitions, and futures. If Jesus is Lord, and we are his servants, we are called not only to think Christ's thoughts and obey his commands but to follow his example of ministry.

I do not hesitate to say that every Christian is called to ministry. I do not say that every Christian is called to *the* ministry, by which is meant the pastoral ministry, but every Christian without any exception whatsoever is called to give his or her life in service. The Greek word for ministry (*diakonia*) means service, and there are many kinds of service. Many may be perplexed about their life's work, not knowing how to discover what it should be. They can certainly begin with this fixed point. All Christians are called to ministry. All Christians are called to give their lives in service. For if Jesus is a servant and we are called to follow him, then we must give our lives in service also. The only difference between us is the precise nature which that service will take. It might be as a pastor; it might be as a missionary; it might be in one of the great professions like law, medicine, education, or the social services; it might be in one of what we sometimes call the more secular spheres—in politics, the mass media, business, or industry; it might be as a wife, mother, and homemaker. There are many forms of Christian ministry, but whatever form it takes, it is ministry, and in it we will be stretched in the service of God and man. Everything we have and are by the creation and redemption of a sovereign God will be used and fulfilled in that ministry.

I once spoke at one of the big department stores in London, and in the question time that followed a young man who was doing very well in this store said to me, "My trouble is that I'm very anxious to get on with my job and get promoted. I'm so anxious to do this that I really have no time to serve Jesus Christ."

I said, "What on earth are you talking about? You are serving Jesus Christ if you're giving yourself to your job. And if you do not see yourself as serving Jesus Christ in your job, you've got no business to be in it." In our work we ought to be giving ourselves to the service of God and man under the lordship of Christ. This is the vocational implication.

An Ecclesiastical Implication

Jesus is Lord of the church. And the church is the community of those who acknowledge Jesus as Lord. The apostle Paul called the church the body of Christ. If the church is the body of Christ, Christ is the head of the body. God has exalted Jesus far above all principality and power, put everything under his feet, and "gave him to be the head over all things to the church" (Eph. 1:22).

When we accept that Jesus is the Lord of the church, the church will be delivered from clericalism. Clericalism is the clerical domination of the laity by which paid clergy keep laypeople under their thumbs and do not allow them to take their responsible part in the work of the church. There are many pastors who behave like that, usurping a headship that belongs to Christ alone. The church's human leaders must never behave in such a way as to deny the headship of Christ.

Jesus introduced a new style of leadership into the world. Jesus said that in the secular community people lord it over one another. They exercise authority over one another and manipulate one another. "Not so with you," Jesus said. "Instead, whoever wants to become great among you must be your servant, and whoever wants to be first must be slave of all" (Mark 6:43–44 NIV). Here is the biblical vision of the true pastor and church leaders. Leadership is not lordship. There must be leadership in the church, but lordship belongs to Christ.

Jesus enlarged on this in Matthew 23, noting how the Pharisees loved to be lords. The Pharisees loved people to bow *to* them and give them deferential titles. They loved to have the chief seats in the synagogue and at the banquets. "But not you," Jesus said. "You're not to call anybody Father, or even teacher in the church." Why not? Well, partly because we are all brothers and sisters, and to give special place to certain members is disruptive of Christian brotherhood. It also usurps the prerogative of the Trinity. We have one Father in heaven, one Lord Jesus Christ, and one Teacher, the Holy Spirit; so we must never offer to another human being that attitude of dependence that we should have toward God alone.

A Political Implication

Jesus is Lord over our life in the secular world. To begin with, our Christian duty is not limited to the church. We who serve the Lord Jesus Christ must take our obedience out into the world where Christ is not acknowledged. The righteousness of the Lord demands not only our individual righteousness. It demands social righteousness as well. This includes the Christian's business ethics and his tax returns, his relationship to his boss or his employees, his understanding of leisure and art and culture, and his attitude to those in authority roles in the community. And this includes his view of politics as well.

Politics is the life of the *polis*, and *polis* is the secular city. *Polis* is the world into which Jesus has sent his people to act as salt and light. This means that the Christian maintains toward the secular culture and state an attitude that is not conformist but critical. In New Testament days, the affirmation "Jesus is Lord" had tremendous political overtones. Some of the caesars in those days demanded divine honors. They expected to be worshipped as God. A zealous procurator would sometimes parade the citizens of a local town into the forum where there was a bust of the Roman emperor with a little fire burning before it, and he would invite the citizens to sprinkle incense on the bust and proclaim, "Caesar is Lord." No Christian would do it. How could he say "Caesar is Lord" when Jesus is Lord? He could not bow down and worship the state or Caesar. To say "Jesus is Lord" is a political affirmation. So these Christians went to prison and death rather than deny his lordship.

What about our own day? Is there any application for us? The issue is more blurred. In the Soviet Union and in some countries of eastern Europe, dominant members of the Orthodox communion have contrived a means of living with the state that seems to many of us to involve compromise. But it ill becomes us to criticize from our long-distance security. Protestant Christians in Marxist regimes are far more vulnerable to persecution because they refuse to conform and insist that their proper stance to the state is one of criticism rather than conformity. In the so-called liberal democracies of the West, there are other totalitarian tyrannies that we Christians often fail to recognize and to which we treacherously bow down and worship. There is the tyrant of consumerism, the tyrant of materialism and material affluence. It is all too easy for us to acquiesce in a civil religion that mistakes the American or European way of life for the Christian way of life and liberally sprinkles the Stars and Stripes (or, if you live in my country, the Union Jack) with holy water. That is civil religion. It is an uncritical bowing down to what is fashionable in the community.

Is there any way in which Christians can commend the lordship of Christ to the non-Christian community? I believe there is. I do not want you to misunderstand me. I am not advocating the old liberal social gospel; I am not trying to rehash it. It is impossible for a biblical Christian to equate social justice with the kingdom of God, for the kingdom of God is not social justice in the secular community. The kingdom of God is a Christological matter. It is only by a personal relationship with Jesus Christ that we can submit to the kingly rule of God and enter the sphere of his kingdom. God's righteousness is fully displayed in God's kingdom alone, that is, among Christian people. But there is a sense in which this righteousness of God can spill over from the Christian community into the world outside.

Let me elaborate for a moment. The church is God's new society. But it is more than that. It is God's new humanity, and God means for the Christian community to demonstrate to the world outside what human community looks like when it comes under the kingly rule of God. In theological terms, this means that the church is the sign of the kingdom. God means the church to exhibit to the wider community outside the true meaning of righteousness, love, freedom, and compassion. If the Christian community demonstrates these attributes as it deals with the secular community, it is acting as society's salt checking decay, and society's light illumining darkness. That is not salvation. That falls far short of redeeming people from sin and judgment. But although it is not salvation, surely we must agree that even among those who do not honor Jesus as Lord,

God prefers love to hate, freedom to oppression, justice to injustice, and peace to strife. It is part of our Christian obedience to Jesus as Lord to seek to promote the standards of Jesus even in the non-Christian community.

A Global Implication

Jesus is Lord of our missionary outreach. Reformed Christians are sometimes criticized for their lack of evangelistic zeal on the ground that belief in God's sovereignty inhibits evangelism. Well, sometimes among Reformed Christians who are not reformed enough—if I may put it like that—this has been true. But I have to say that evangelistic apathy is not part of the Reformed faith. On the contrary, it is our sovereign Lord Jesus claiming all authority in heaven and earth who sends us and commissions us to go into the world to preach the gospel and make disciples, and it is under the authority of this sovereign Lord that we do so. This is the global implication of the lordship of Jesus. Preaching the gospel is the very means that God has ordained to bring his elect to faith in Jesus Christ.

Demand for Allegiance

The lordship of Christ is the most powerful of all missionary incentives. Hindus talk about the Lord Krishna, Buddhists about the Lord Buddha. But we cannot accept them as comparable to the Lord Jesus, for Jesus is God and Savior and they are not. He will not share his glory with another. It was for the sake of his name, in order that due honor be given to the name of Jesus, that all the early missionaries went out. It is for the sake of that same name that we preach the gospel. We long that Jesus should be acknowledged as Lord.

The study of doctrine at Reformed conferences is a very perilous occupation. It is even more so when the object of our study is Jesus as Lord, for it is impossible to study Jesus Christ with cool and detached objectivity. The One we study together has a disconcerting way of refusing to remain an object of scrutiny. He transforms himself from an object of scrutiny into a subject who scrutinizes us. He has a disturbing way of insisting on being precisely what we have been studying: our Lord. The Lord Jesus confronts us now. The Lord Jesus challenges us, the Lord Jesus who alone has authority to bestow salvation upon us and alone has authority to demand our unconditional allegiance.

During the coronation of Her Majesty the Queen in Westminster Abbey, there was a moving scene just before the actual moment when the crown was placed upon her head. The Archbishop of Canterbury as the chief citizen in the country called four times toward each point of the compass—north, south, east, and west—saying, "I present unto you the undoubted queen of this realm. Are you willing to do her homage?" Not until a great affirmative shout had thundered down the nave of Westminster Abbey four times was the crown brought out and placed upon her head. And so I say to you, "I present unto you Jesus Christ as your undoubted King and Lord. Are you willing to do him homage?"

2

The "Five Points" and God's Sovereignty

ROGER R. NICOLE

THE FIVE points of Calvinism come to us today in a form that is quite traditional: total depravity, unconditional election, limited atonement, irresistible grace, and perseverance of the saints. But we are not to think that this is the only form the doctrines of grace can take or that the phrases themselves are unalterable. The advantage of this particular formulation is that when you take the first letter of each of these points and read them from top to bottom, you find the word *tulip* and so have an acrostic. The tulip is a beautiful flower, marvelously cultivated in the Netherlands, and since there are many Calvinists in the Netherlands, it seems to be a delightful arrangement to organize these doctrines in terms of the letters of this word. However, I would like to consider the nature of the points and suggest certain rewordings that, in my judgment, may prevent misunderstandings.

Pervasive Evil

The first point is *total depravity*. The purpose of this point is to emphasize that man does not have the ability to please God or even to come to him in salvation unless God moves him to it. This turns attention away from man in his action and ability and instead directs it toward God and his sovereign action. The advantage of expressing this truth in this way is that we emphasize the fundamental and pervasive character of the evil in man.

The terms that are used are somewhat misleading, however. I find that invariably, after having said "total depravity," the staunchest Calvinists find it important to qualify this phrase. They add, "But we don't mean to say by this that man is quite as bad as he could be." Practically everybody who says "total depravity" or "total inability" has to qualify this at once.

Obviously, people who seek to know what Calvinism is ought to make it their business to examine not only the five familiar phrases but also the meanings behind those phrases. But since those words are used repeatedly, we cannot blame inquirers too harshly for taking them at face value. Nor can we blame them when, thinking that Calvinists believe every man is as evil as he can be, these people point to virtuous, praiseworthy men and ask, "How can you hold to your Calvinism in the presence of this?" Perhaps it would be wiser to simply use a different phrase that would emphasize the indispensable character of this divine grace and would not need so quickly to have a qualification.

May I suggest that what the Calvinist wishes to say when he speaks of total depravity is that evil is at the very heart and root of man. It is at the very foundation, at the deepest level of human life. This evil does not corrupt merely one or two or certain particular avenues of the life of man but is pervasive in that it spreads into all aspects of his life. It darkens his mind, corrupts his feelings, warps his will, moves his affections in wrong directions, blinds his conscience, burdens his subconscious, afflicts his body. There is hardly any dimension of man in which the damaging character of evil does not manifest itself in some way. Evil is like a root cancer that extends in all directions within the organism to leave its devastating effects.

How shall we express this? Well, I am not too happy about my substitutions, but I would like to suggest that the term be *radical depravity* or *pervasive depravity*. This is a little less sweeping than *total* and, in that sense, a little closer to what we really want to assert.

Divine Initiative

The second point is *unconditional election*. The emphasis here is upon the fact that it is God who takes the initiative. There is no merit or condition in the creature, either present or foreseen, that determines the divine choice. This is the key to what is in view.

The disadvantage to this formulation is twofold. In the first place, it is not sufficiently comprehensive, for it suggests that the only thing that God does is to elect people to be saved and that, therefore, there is no relationship of God to those who are lost. But election not only involves the taking of some to be saved; it also involves the bypassing of the remainder of mankind and the just reprobation of them in view of their sins. So just to talk of election is not enough. We should also recognize preterition, the bypassing of those who are not to be saved.

Moreover, the term *unconditional* might be misconstrued to suggest that God has no interest in the condition of those whom he chooses to make his redeemed people. It suggests that God is not concerned about what we are, what we become, and how we relate ourselves to his will. We are correct if we understand the term *unconditional* to mean that God does not base his choice on the relative merits of the elect. But if we assume that God does not care about the condition of those whom he has chosen to save, we are wholly incorrect. For the Scripture makes it very clear that we are elected "unto good works, which God has before ordained that we should walk in them" (Eph. 2:10).

What we need to recognize here is that the sovereign initiative in salvation is with God. It is not with man. God does not save a man by virtue of something that God has foreseen in him, some preexisting condition that is the source or root of God's elective purpose. In his own sovereign wisdom, God chooses those who shall be saved, for reasons that are sufficient unto himself. We may, therefore, much better speak of the sovereign election and preterition of God.

Particular Redemption

Then comes the third point, which is sometimes called *limited atonement*. This, I think, is a complete misnomer. The other points I can live with, but *limited atonement* I cannot live with, for it is a total misrepresentation of what we mean to say.

The purpose of using this expression is to say that the atonement is not universal: Christ did not die for every member of the race in the same sense in which he died for those who will be redeemed. Therefore, the purpose of the atonement is restricted to the elect and is not spread to the universality of mankind.

Some limit the atonement in breadth; that is, they say the Lord Jesus Christ died for the redeemed and that he sees to it that the redeemed are therefore saved. Those who hold this view say there is a certain group of mankind, a particular group, that is the special object of the redemptive love and substitutionary work of Jesus Christ. The remainder of mankind may gain some benefits from the work of Christ, but they are not encompassed in his design in the same way that the elect are. This is one way of limiting the scope of the atonement.

Other people say that Christ died for everybody in the same way, but that some of the people for whom Christ died are at the end lost. In this view, the death of Christ does not, in fact, insure the salvation of all those for whom he died. The effect is to limit the depth of the atonement. The atonement is ineffective. It does not secure the salvation of all the people for whom it is intended. The will of God and the redemptive love of Jesus Christ are frustrated by the wicked will of men who resist him and do not accept his grace. According to this view, salvation consists of the work of Christ together with the acceptance, or nonresistance, or some ingredient of one kind or another that some people add, and it is *this* ingredient that really constitutes the difference between being saved and being lost. No one who says that at the end there will be some people saved and other people lost can in honesty speak of an unlimited atonement.

For these reasons, I am not happy to go under the banner of a limited atonement, as though Calvinists wickedly emasculate and mutilate the great scope and beauty of the love and redemption of Jesus Christ. For it is not a question of limits. It is a question of purpose.

How should we therefore phrase it? We ought rather to talk about *definite atonement.* We ought to say that there was a definite purpose of Christ in offering himself. The substitution was not a blanket substitution. It was a substitution that was oriented specifically to the purpose for which he came into this world, namely, to save and redeem those whom the Father has given him. Another term that is appropriate, although perhaps less precise than *definite atonement*, is *particular redemption.*

For the redemption of Christ is a particular redemption that accomplished what it purposed. The only alternative is that Christ redeemed no one in particular.

If we change the language in this way, I think we spare ourselves the charge of restricting the scope of the love of Christ. If I say that my position is that of limited atonement, my opponent will say, "You believe in limited atonement, but I believe in unlimited atonement." He seems to be the one who exalts the grace of God. But see what happens when we use my words. I say, "I believe in a definite atonement." What can my opponent say? "I believe in an indefinite atonement"? If I use the old language, I have no opportunity to do anything except protest. If I use the new language, I do not put myself at a psychological disadvantage from the start. Incidentally, the term *definite atonement* is found in the writings of men like John Owen and William Cunningham of Scotland. So let us abandon the expression *limited atonement*, which disfigures the Calvinistic doctrine of grace in the work of Christ.

Effectual Grace

The fourth point is *irresistible grace*. The emphasis here is upon the fact that God accomplishes his designs, so that the saving grace of God cannot be resisted unto perdition. But a misunderstanding may also arise from this phrase, for it may suggest that a man can resist to the very end and that God will nevertheless press him willy-nilly, kicking and screaming, into the kingdom. This is not the case. The grace of God does not function against our wills but is rather a grace that overcomes the resistance of our wills. God the Holy Spirit is able to accomplish this.

But how can God the Holy Spirit accomplish this without violating free will and making us into puppets? I do not know how he can do it, but that is what he does. I am not concerned about God's modes of operation, and I am quite ready to grant that he may well have a good number that I do not know about and that I am not able to explore. I do know that when there is resistance God comes in with his mighty grace and subdues that resistance. He makes no one come against his will, but he makes him willing to come. He does not do violence to the will of the creature, but he gently subdues and overcomes human resistance so that men will gladly respond to him and come in repentance and faith. We ought not to give the impression that somehow God forces himself upon his creatures so that the gospel is crammed down their throats, as it were.

In the case of adults, it is always in keeping with the willingness of the individual that the response to grace comes forth. This is surely apparent in the case of the apostle Paul, for whom God had made what might perhaps be called the maximum effort to bring him in. He resisted, but God overcame his resistance. The result is that Paul was brought willingly and happily into the fold of the grace of God. What we mean here is not *irresistible*—which gives the impression that man continues to resist—but *effectual*. That is, the grace of God actually accomplishes what he intends it to accomplish.

God's Perseverance

The last point is called the *perseverance of the saints*, and the emphasis is that those who have been won by the grace of God will not lose out but will be preserved by God's grace to ultimate salvation. It means that it is not possible for one who is truly regenerate to fall out of the reach of divine grace, lose salvation altogether, and finally be lost.

The advantage of this formulation is that there is indeed a human activity in this process. The saints are active. They are not passive. In a true sense they are called upon to persevere. But there is a devastating weakness in this formulation in that it suggests that the key to this perseverance is the activity of the saints. It suggests that they persevere because they are strong, that they are finally saved because they show that kind of stability and consistency that prevents them from turning back into their original wickedness. This is never the case. The key to perseverance is the preservation by God of his saints, that is, the stability of his purpose and the fixity of his design. What is to be in view here is not so much the perseverance of those who are saved but the perseverance of God with the sinners whom he has gloriously transformed and whom he assists to the end. We ought to talk about God's perseverance with his saints. That is the proper emphasis.

A New Acrostic?

We now need to review our terms: *radical depravity*, *sovereign election and preterition*, *definite atonement*, *effectual grace*, and the *perseverance of God with his saints*. Those are the terms I suggested. Unfortunately, the terms do not provide acrostics in English, French, German, Latin, or any other language I know of. So we have lost our TULIP, that beautiful mnemonic device to help us remember these five points in a simple manner. On the one hand, I think it may be preferable to lose it, if those other terms mislead people as to what it is we actually hold. We certainly do not want to sell our birthright, which is the truth, for a mess of pottage, which is an acrostic.

On the other hand, I do not want to finish on this note. So I would like to suggest to you that there is a way in which we ought to unite the five points—for in a very special sense we ought to recognize that the five points of Calvinism are, in reality, not five separate doctrines that we assert almost as disjointed elements but rather articulation of one point, which is the grace of God. Total depravity we may call *indispensable grace*. It is the truth that without God's grace we can do nothing good because we are so evil. Election, called in Scripture the election of grace, may well be called *differentiating grace* or *sovereign grace*. Definite atonement is *provision-making grace*, for it refers to that grace by which God has established a basis for salvation. The fourth point is *effectual* or *efficacious grace*. Perseverance of the saints may be called *indefectible grace*, grace that will never fail us. In this way we can see how the points simply formulate what Scripture presents to us concerning God's grace.

If you want to, you can make an acrostic that reads GOSPEL. The G would be *grace*; the O, total depravity, would be *obligatory grace*; the S would be *sovereign grace*; the P, corresponding to definite atonement, would be *provision-making grace*; the E would be *effectual grace*; finally, the L would be *lasting grace*. I do not like this as well as I like my other terms, so I present it with some diffidence. But if you are hung up on an acrostic, use it. At any rate, get something that has more meaning than TULIP.

Even better, let us go to the heart of the gospel and say, "Calvinism is the gospel," and then spell it out. This is what the Reformed position is all about, after all. *Sola gratia!* By grace alone! That is what we are talking about. The five points of Calvinism merely conjoin to this. Moreover, we do not even have to go to the Reformation; we can go directly to the Scripture.

Here is a text: Jonah 2:9. It reads, "Salvation is of the LORD." And, in the New Scofield Bible, which I will venture to quote, there is a beautiful little note on that text that says, "The theme of the Scripture." That is exactly it. Salvation is of the Lord! That is the theme of Scripture and of the five points of Calvinism.

3

The Doctrines of Grace in Jesus's Teaching

ROGER R. NICOLE

DOES CALVINISM find support in the teachings of our Lord Jesus Christ? Or, to put it differently, are there statements that Christ made that give evidence of the doctrines of sovereign grace, those doctrines that have been the center of Reformed thought?

When we raise the question "Is there support in the teachings of our Lord for the tenets of Calvinism, for the doctrines of sovereign grace?" we do not suggest that if by any chance there were no support these tenets would therefore be false. Our Lord did not indicate that he taught us everything, as though the whole substance of Christian doctrine should be found in his words rather than in Scripture as a whole. We recognize that the whole Bible is to be the norm of our faith, not merely that portion of it that is found in red in our red-letter New Testaments. At the same time, however, it is also true that the statements of our Lord are especially dear to our hearts. So obviously what he thought important to present to his apostles and to convey to us through their pen is of paramount significance among those who are Christians.

Furthermore, in some cases these teachings might find acceptance in places where other portions of Scripture might be rejected. In some quarters of Christendom, we find people who say, "I do not care what Paul said; show me what Jesus taught." Or some people may be so bold as to say, "Paul erred on this thing." Or again, "Paul was a male chauvinist; I want to stick with the statements of the Lord Jesus Christ." So while we are quite ready to recognize that in God's own providence the whole of the Bible is normative for us, it is true that sometimes it is valuable to check precisely what Jesus himself taught and attempt to synthesize his message.

You may wonder whether there is much that Jesus said that relates to the doctrines of sovereign grace, and I suppose that I am going to stun you here with some statistics. I went to the New Testament to read again everything that Jesus said—all 1,780 verses. And I will confess to you that I was dumbfounded to find how very many passages actually relate to this topic. From the notes that I have, I judge that there are about five hundred verses that contain some reference to the doctrines of grace—almost one-third of what our Lord is recorded as saying. These verses relate to the evil in man that calls for grace, to the sovereign rights of God, to his wonderful provision whereby the Lord has given himself for the redemption of sinners, to the power of the Holy Spirit to attract sinners, and to God's power to safeguard them to the end so that they will finally rejoice forever in the fellowship of their Lord.

So the doctrines of grace are not relegated to a meager section of the teaching of Jesus. This is not an area where we have to cast our net again and again like poor Peter and find it coming back empty. Almost any place at all that you cast your net, you will find some statements of our Lord about grace.

You will find them in Matthew, Mark, and Luke—and you will find them in great abundance in John. John perhaps better than anyone understood the Lord Jesus. His gospel is veritably filled with statements of our Lord that magnify the grace of God.

An Evil Generation

One of these points, total depravity, emphasizes especially the utter need in which man is bound and that calls for the grace of God. The grace of God has to be manifested because man is totally helpless, because he is unable to lift himself in any way toward heaven. This does not mean that he is fully as bad as he could possibly be. This does not mean that you cannot find some little good in some men here and there. But it means that in relationship to salvation man is dead, depraved, and lost.

Our Lord Jesus Christ, with all the concern, compassion, and love that he showed to mankind, made some very vivid portrayals of man's condition. He did not mince words about the gravity of human sin. He talked of man as salt that has lost its savor (Matt. 5:13). He talked of man as a corrupt tree that is bound to produce corrupt fruit (Matt. 7:17). He talked of man as being evil: "You then, being evil, know how to give good gifts to your children" (Luke 11:13). On one occasion he lifted up his eyes toward heaven and talked about an "evil and adulterous generation" (Matt. 12:39), or again, "this wicked generation" (v. 45). In a great passage dealing with what constitutes true impurity and true purity, he made the startling statement that out of the heart proceed murders, adulteries, evil thoughts, and things of that kind (Mark 7:21–23). He spoke about Moses having to give special permissive commandments to men because of the hardness of their hearts (Matt. 19:8). When the rich young ruler approached him, saying, "Good Master," Jesus said, "There is none good but . . . God" (Mark 10:18). In this, incidentally, he did not mean to deny that he himself was good but, rather, he wanted to rebuke the man for the glibness with which he was using the term *good*. The man was not ready to recognize the one he addressed as God.

Jesus compared men, even the leaders of his country, to wicked servants in a vineyard (Matt. 21:33–41). He exploded in condemnation of the scribes and the Pharisees, who were considered to be among the best men, men who were in the upper ranges of virtue and in the upper classes of society (Matt. 23:2–39).

The Lord Jesus made a fundamental statement about man's depravity in John 3:6: "That which is born of the flesh is flesh." He saw in man an unwillingness to respond to grace: "You will not come" (John 5:40), "You have not the love of God" (v. 42), "You receive me not" (v. 43), "You believe not" (v. 47). Such sayings occur repeatedly in the gospel of John: "The works [of the world] are evil" (John 7:7); "None of you keeps the law" (v. 19). "[You] shall die in your sins," he says (John 8:21). "You are from beneath" (v. 23); "You are of your father the devil . . . a murderer . . . [and] a liar" (v. 44); "You are not of God" (v. 47); "You are not of my sheep" (John 10:26); "He that hates me hates my Father" (John 15:23). This is the way in which our Lord spoke to the leaders of the Jews. He brought to the fore their utter inability to please God.

Following another line of approach, he showed also the blindness of man, that is, his utter inability to know God and understand him. Here again we have a whole series of passages showing that no man knows the Father but him to whom the Son has revealed him (Matt. 11:27). He compared men to the blind leading the blind (Matt. 15:14). He mentioned that Jerusalem itself did not know or understand the purpose of God and, as a result, disregarded the things that concern salvation

(Luke 19:42). The Gospel of John records him as saying that he that believed not was condemned already because he had not believed on the Son of God (John 3:18). "This is the condemnation, that . . . men loved darkness rather than light, because their deeds were evil" (v. 19). He said that only the one who has been reached by grace can walk not in darkness but have the light of life (John 8:12). The Lord Jesus emphasized that it is essential for man to be saved by a mighty act of God if he is to be rescued from his condition of misery (John 3:3, 5, 7–16). Even in the Lord's Prayer, the Lord teaches us to say, "Forgive us our debts" (Matt. 6:12). And this is a prayer that we need to repeat again and again. He said that the sick, not the whole, are the people who need a physician (Matt. 9:12). We are those sick people who need a physician to help us and redeem us. He said that we are people who are burdened and heavy-laden (Matt. 11:28). In him alone can we find rest. "Except you be converted," he said, ". . . you shall not enter into the kingdom of heaven" (Matt. 18:3). He represents the situation of man as that of a debtor who had nothing by which he could absolve his debts (v. 25). He tells us in the great parables of Luke 15 that our soul is like a child so estranged that he has forfeited any right to belong to the family of God.

Here again in John the message comes with particular pungency: "Except a man be born of water and of the Spirit, he cannot enter into the kingdom of God" (John 3:5). And once more, "You must be born again" (v. 7). There is a necessity here not only of some reformation or adjustment, not only of some repainting of old walls, but a total renewal that starts at the very roots of the personality. Therefore, he says that the one who knows him has passed from death unto life. "No man can come to me, except the Father . . . draw him" (John 6:44; see also v. 65). "Except you eat the flesh of the Son of man, and drink his blood, you have no life in you" (v. 53). He compares the situation of man to those who are in slavery and bondage (John 8:34), and he says that only in himself can one find freedom. "The truth shall make you free" (v. 32); "If the Son therefore shall make you free, you shall be free indeed" (v. 36)—that is, unless the Son makes you free you remain slaves indeed. "Without me," he said, "you can do nothing" (John 15:5).

The people who were most readily received by the Lord were those who had this sense of need and who therefore did not come to him with a sense of the sufficiency of their performance. The people he received were those who came brokenhearted and bruised with the sense of their inadequacy.

Surely this is the meaning of the great parable of the Pharisee and the publican (Luke 18:9–14). On the one hand, judging by external standards, the Pharisee was head and shoulders above the publican, who had probably been dishonest in raising the taxes of others. The Pharisee did not have that defect, but in coming to God he was not lifting his prayer higher than the roof. He was praying within himself. On the other hand, the publican said, "Have mercy upon me, O Lord. I do not deserve any consideration or any help. I am depraved. I am helpless. Have mercy on me." The Lord Jesus said that he, rather than the other, went to his home justified (v. 14).

This again is beautifully represented in the parable of the prodigal son, who said, "[I] am no more worthy to be called your son" (Luke 15:21).

God's Power

Not only does the doctrine of grace tell us about the great need of man, but it also tells us about the great ability of God to respond to that need. The Lord Jesus Christ has exalted the sovereign power of God. He has represented God as capable of doing anything he pleases. He has shown that he is the one who exercises judgment over the whole world. He sustains even the flights of little birds by his almighty power (Matt. 10:29). He is the one who appoints the destinies of individuals and nations. He is the one who is capable of healing men with one word (Matt. 8:8). "With God," says the Lord Jesus, "all things are possible" (Matt. 19:26). With man it is impossible. It is impossible that a rich man, for instance, should come into the kingdom, but with God all things are possible.

Therefore the Lord Jesus Christ encouraged his disciples to look to God with confidence. He did not say, "Watch out that you do not ask God something that is too difficult for him. Just show a little restraint in your prayer and adjust your request to the powers and provisions that God has at his command." He said nothing of the kind! He said, "The sky is the limit! Go right ahead and ask what you want, in my name, submitting your will to the will of God and trusting that God is able to move mountains to manifest his sovereign mastery of the universe" (Matt. 21:22). Even in his address to Pilate, the Lord made that very plain. He said to Pilate, the powerful Roman governor, "You could have no power at all against me, except it were given you from above" (John 19:11).

Our Lord did not suggest that we are to introduce qualifications by saying, "Well, God's power is limited by the ability of man to resist. The free will of man needs to be taken into consideration and may sharply curtail what God is able to accomplish." There are no limits to what God can accomplish. Though our Lord recognized the reality of human agency, rationality, and freedom, he never presented these as introducing a restriction or a qualification on the sovereign power of God. Thus Christ taught not only sovereign power but sovereign decision as well. The decisions of God embrace the destinies of men. They are decisions that are granted in his good pleasure and are not always dependent on what you might call the ability of man to respond. For instance, the Lord Jesus shows that there were people who might very well have benefited by his ministry but who were not privileged to receive it. He says that Sodom and Gomorrah would have repented if they had been exposed to his ministry, but they did not get it. He says that Tyre and Sidon would have repented if they had been privileged to see the kind of miracles which Capernaum and Bethsaida saw, but they did not receive such a vision (Matt. 11:21–24).

Why is it that God did not give to these people the blessing that he bestowed on others? No answer is forthcoming. Our Lord does not feel that God must account to us why he does one thing or another. Everything he does in the area of salvation is purely of grace. What we deserve at his hand is condemnation. So, rather than say, "How come, Lord, that you do not do for me as much as you do for somebody else?" we should come to him and say, "How wonderful, O Lord, that in your mercy you have not allowed me to perish in my sin and rebellion, which amply deserved any condemnation that I would have received from you."

This, I think, is the drastic error that our Pelagian friends are making. They speak as if man had a right to come into the presence of God and enter into account with him, as if God had some obligation to deal with all people in the same way. The one thing God owes us is judgment. We ought to marvel at the fact that instead of confining us all to judgment and damnation, God in his mercy has been pleased to make plans to save a great multitude. He has caused them to hear the gospel, receive forgiveness in Jesus Christ, be drawn in faith and repentance by the Holy Spirit to respond to the offer of the gospel, and be preserved to the end so that they will spend eternity in the blessed presence and fellowship of God. This is the marvelous truth. The fact that this has not been done for the whole of the race does not provide us with a proper ground for recrimination.

This is plain from the attitude of our Lord. Christ expresses precisely this principle in that great parable of the workers of the vineyard. He makes the owner of the vineyard say, "My friend, I do you no harm. Am I not free to do with my property what I please? And if I want to pay somebody who has worked only one hour as much as somebody else who has worked twelve hours, that is up to me, as long as I have not defrauded you in the salary that we had arranged together" (see Matt. 20:13–15). This parable causes some difficulty, but it is a parable of Jesus. And in this parabolic teaching, our Lord shows us that we have no proper ground to recriminate against God for what may appear to us at times to be his arbitrary decisions.

God's perfection includes wisdom. So nothing that God does is without an appropriate ground. But we do not always have to know what that ground is. In this we should be like children. Once in a while children ought to obey without knowing for what reason the parents give a commandment; otherwise they do not really obey the commandment—they obey the reason. So do we need to be submitted to God's sovereign decisions.

The Lord Jesus speaks frequently of the elect. An example is John 15:16: "You have not chosen me, but I have chosen you, and ordained you, that you should go and bring forth fruit, and that your fruit should remain." Some say this is not election to salvation; rather, it is an election to service. Perhaps. But there is more in the statement of our Lord than simply the question of who is called to service. In a true sense there is sovereign determination of who can *hear* the Word of God, for the Lord said that no man can come "except the Father . . . draw him" (John 6:44).

In all this our Lord never dismissed the reality of human freedom. That is explicit even in regard to the great passage just quoted: "You have not chosen me, but I have chosen you." The disciples would have considered this literally true. They had not made application in triplicate to be included in the College of the Apostles or answered fifty-five questions on five different copies in order to become citizens in Christ's kingdom. No, in every case Christ took the initiative. He saw Peter and Andrew fishing and said, "Follow me, and I will make you fishers of men" (Matt. 4:19). He saw Matthew at his tax table and said, "Follow me" (Matt. 9:9). Every one of the disciples came into that position by the direct initiative of Christ. But notice—this did not obliterate their wills. None of those people was mandated by a policeman. None was dragged willy-nilly behind our Lord in his journeys. They came of their own will. They came willingly. The Lord did not make them go against their will; he made them willing to go.

So the reality of God's action does not preempt the reality of our free agency. The kind of Calvinism that dismisses the reality of freedom of agency is a truncated Calvinism. It is not true Calvinism because it is not truly biblical. We need to recognize that God does not deal with man as pieces of wood, iron, inanimate matter, puppets, or anything of that kind; he deals with man in terms of the rational agency that he himself has created and that to some extent reflects his wonderful image.

Definite Atonement

Not only does Christ talk about election to salvation, but, in his dealings with Judas, he gives us some inkling of that dark and difficult doctrine of reprobation. He said that he had lost no one except "the son of perdition," that the Scripture should be fulfilled (John 17:12). The Scripture is very sober about this. Never does it suggest for even one moment that the ground of reprobation is some arbitrary condemnation by God. The ground of reprobation is always the sin of man and yet, ultimately, there is a sense in which God has made the sovereign decision as to who will be elect and who will be reproved.

This is echoed in the words of our Lord. The Lord Jesus Christ emphasized that the atonement he was to offer is related in a special way to those who are redeemed. The Lord said that the Son of Man came to give his life as a ransom for *many*, not for *all* (Mark 10:45). He repeated this in the institution of the Lord's Supper: "This [cup] is my blood of the new testament, which is shed for many for the remission of sins" (Matt. 26:28). In John he said, "I am come that [the sheep] might have life. . . . The good shepherd gives his life for the sheep" (John 10:10–11). And in the immediate context he makes the distinction between those who are his sheep and those who are not his sheep (v. 26).

If that is not enough, note that our Lord expressly rejects the universal reference in at least one of his prayers, for he says, "I pray not for the world, but for those you have given me" (John 17:9).

It is true that our Lord also recognizes some benevolence of God toward creation at large. He talks to us about the Father who makes his sun rise on the wicked as well as the good (Matt. 5:45). He talks about the fact that it is not the will of the Father in heaven that "one of these little ones should perish" (Matt. 18:14). He says that God is kind, even to the unthankful (Luke 6:35). He says, "Be you therefore merciful, as your Father also is merciful" (v. 36). He says, "The bread that I will give is my flesh, which I will give for the life of the world" (John 6:51); "I . . . will draw all men unto me" (John 12:32). He says, "God so loved the world, that he gave his only begotten Son, that whosoever believes in him should not perish, but have everlasting life" (John 3:16). So there is a sense in which there is reference to the wide concern of God. Yet when the question is raised, "For whom did our Lord design to give himself as a ransom and as a substitution?" the answer must be, "For those who will, in fact, be saved and whose redemption has, in fact, been secured by the death of our Lord."

Effectual Grace

The Lord Jesus spoke about the effectiveness of the grace of God: "This is the work of God, that you believe on him whom he has sent" (John 6:29); "All that the Father gives me shall come to me" (v. 37); "No man can come to me, except the Father who has sent me draw him: and I will raise him up at the last day" (v. 44); "Every man . . . who has heard, and has learned of the Father, comes unto me" (v. 45). God has ways to make his grace effective. He can overcome the resistance of our wicked hearts and can lead us willingly to repentance and faith so that we embrace the grace that is offered to us.

Lasting Grace

In closing, the question arises: Does this grace, when it is once received, continue? Is it lasting, or can it vanish? Can our sins eclipse the benefits of the grace of God? Can those who have once been redeemed fall again into perdition, out of the range of divine blessing and back into the clutches of Satan?

Here again our Lord has most significant statements to make. He talks about the way in which the seed that is cast into good ground grows unto harvest (Matt. 13:23). He talks about gathering the wheat into the barn and throwing away the tares (v. 30). (The wheat represents the children of the kingdom.) He talks about the fact that the gates of hell shall not prevail against the building of the church of Jesus Christ (Matt. 16:18). He tells us that Satan would deceive the elect if it were possible, but the implication clearly is that it is not possible (Matt. 24:24). He speaks about giving everlasting life (John 10:28). What kind of everlastingness would end in this brief course of our pilgrimage? He says that he who believes in him shall never thirst (John 4:14). How could that be if, in the end, in rejection of God we could consign ourselves once again to damnation? He says that this is the will of the Father that he should lose no one, but rather raise them up at the last day (John 6:39). He says that the Lord holds his sheep—that no one shall take them out of his hand, that they shall never perish, that he gives them eternal life (John 10:28).

What kind of a shepherd would say, "All I care about is to be sure that the wolves do not come in and damage the flock. So I let the sheep wander as they wish. When some of them get lost, I say to the owner, 'Well, I can't help it; they got lost by themselves'"? One of the tasks of the shepherd is to be sure that the sheep do not get lost. If they do get lost, then there are accounts to be settled. The Lord Jesus is the Good Shepherd. He is not going to allow his sheep to wander away. That, in fact, is expressly stated. He gives them *eternal life*. They shall *never perish*. So it is not correct to say, "Well, no one can snatch them out of his hand, but they can jump—and if they jump, they perish." Our Lord's teaching clearly contradicts this.

However, there are warnings in our Lord's statements. He says that the one who perseveres to the end shall be saved (Matt. 24:13). He says that the servant will be blessed whom the Lord finds watching (v. 46). He gives us the parable of the ten virgins in which there are people who seem to be related to the wedding but who, in the end, do not have a share in the celebration because somehow they fall asleep at the wrong time (Matt. 25:1–13). He talks of others as unprofitable servants who, at the time of distribution, are cast out where there is weeping and gnashing of teeth (v. 30). He gives us the example of Judas, who, even though one of the apostles, seemed to withdraw and perish (Matt. 26:24). He tells us in John 15 that every branch that does not bear fruit he takes away (v. 2). So our Lord does not encourage us to take the benefits of his grace for granted. The doctrine of security is not meant to encourage a false security in people who are eager to do evil. It is a doctrine that is meant to encourage the confidence of the child of God in the sufficiency of the care, watchfulness, and perseverance of his heavenly Father.

Thus every one of the great points of Calvinism finds direct support in the words of Jesus. Some of them find no better support anywhere else in Scripture. Did Jesus teach Calvinism? Was Jesus a Calvinist? Would the Author of all grace teach us concerning the doctrines of grace? Why, certainly! And it is our comfort and refuge.

The one who taught us so eloquently about grace is the one who sits on the throne of grace to intercede for his own, to lift them up in the presence of the Father so that God's blessing may rest upon them (Heb. 4:16). Listen to the words of Jesus. First, John 6:44: "No man can come to me, except the Father which hath sent me draw him: and I will raise him up at the last day." Then again, John 10:27–30: "My sheep hear my voice, and I know them, and they follow me: And I give unto them eternal life; and they shall never perish, neither shall any man pluck them out of my hand. My Father, which gave them me, is greater than all; and no man is able to pluck them out of my Father's hand. I and my Father are one." This is the doctrine of grace from the lips of Jesus Christ.

4

God's Sovereignty and Old Testament Names for God

STUART D. SACKS

PERSONAL NAMES in the Old Testament were designed to communicate something distinctive about the individual or his circumstances. Students of Scripture are well aware of the significance attached to names like Abraham and Jacob. Moreover, the change in Abram's name to Abraham, and Jacob's name to Israel, marked great epochs in the lives of these patriarchs. On occasion an Old Testament name spoke of conditions surrounding a child's birth, as in the name Ichabod (1 Sam. 4:21). On other occasions, the names of children expressed parental hopes for their offspring (Gen. 35:18).

It is a superior being, in exercise of his prerogatives, that produces names for other beings. Adam named the creatures, defining them with names suiting their nature and actions. Yet the names that humans affix to others convey depth only insofar as God himself inspirationally motivates such procedure. Moreover, if God led the Jews to identify their fellows with deeply significant names, we should well expect that the Creator, in telling us his names, would also convey something of depth concerning his nature.

The names to be considered here are not names that man gives to God but rather names that God ascribes to himself. Certain divine names are predominant in different periods of revelation, yet such circumscribed usages do not, as some assert, throw suspicion upon the Mosaic authorship of the Pentateuch. They do serve to describe the spiritual significance of a given period. *El Shaddai*, for example, "the Almighty God," is the most common revelation of God in the patriarchal period. Why? Because the patriarchs desperately needed the assurance that such a powerful name provided. We must keep in mind, however, that the Old Testament does not dwell upon what men thought about God. It centers upon what God, in infinite condescension, made known to men.

A Sovereign God

Exodus 20:7 implies that all scriptural names identifying God are to be held in sacred awe. Such a command would be presumptuous were it not uttered by the most supreme being. The diversified pattern of Old Testament divine names confirms the fact of God's absolute supremacy, his sovereignty. We generally refer to the Bible as the Word of God. More appropriately we might refer to it as the "acts of God." These acts reveal one who directs all things after the counsel of his own will.

Present-day conditions cry out for a vital proclamation of God's mighty and limitless dominion. The prophet Daniel said, "And he changes the times and the seasons: he removes kings, and sets up kings" (Dan. 2:21). Later, in the fourth chapter, he wrote, "The most High rules in the kingdom of men, and gives it to whomsoever he will, and sets up over it the basest of men. . . . And all the inhabitants of the earth are reputed as nothing: and he does according to his will in the army of heaven, and among the inhabitants of the earth: and none can stay his hand, or say unto him, What are you doing?" (Dan. 4:17, 35).

The expression "the sovereignty of God" grew out of ancient eastern societies where the king was truly sovereign. The nucleus of political life was the king, for whose sake the state and citizens existed. He held absolute power over his subjects, and all property was under his aegis. He was the supreme authority, the maker and enforcer of every law. Mercy, justice, wrath, and fury were his to display as he found fit. Thus, in Genesis 2:16, as the Lord God places a command upon man, the authority with which he speaks immediately witnesses to his sovereignty. The trees of the garden are his, and man may partake of them only by permission of the owner. The matter admits no prerogative for man; he is at the disposal of the one who issues the command.

While many of the Semitic peoples used *melek* ("king") to identify the deity, only the people of Israel were to learn of the reality of God's sovereignty in an indisputable manner, that is, through his supernatural interposition as king of their nation. In Isaiah 33:22, God is beheld as both lawgiver and administrator of the law. While this concept does not commend itself to us from a purely political standpoint, it is of vital necessity in the kingdom of God. An absolute monarchy is the only viable principle for a truly theocratic government. Man's failure to understand the sovereignty of God stems from the creature's self-directed theology, by which he prefers his own subjective impressions to those of God's Word.

It is hardly possible to study the sovereignty of God apart from those attributes defined as omnipotence, omniscience, and omnipresence. These qualities, in fact, frame essential parts of the picture of the sovereignty of God. It is God's omnipotence that guarantees his sovereignty in the manifestation of might; it is his omniscience that determines the delegation of authority to men; it is his omnipresence that sees to the appropriation of mercy and grace. When man comprehends that God is God, the individual rests on a firm foundation for the experience of God's person. Far from being abstract knowledge for its own sake, a correct conception of God's sovereignty is itself a mode of honoring and glorifying God. As our conception of him is elevated, we will be humbled into submission to his will, relying solely upon him for the great work of salvation and the security he can uniquely provide. As we better understand his sovereignty, we cannot help but praise and glorify him more realistically.

No man motivated God to reveal his name. Seven out of every twelve references to the name of God declare it as *qedosh* ("holy"). In other words, he is unapproachable. He cannot be encountered by sinful man apart from some extraordinary gracious provision emanating from himself. Therefore, that we should know his name reveals God's volitional self-disclosure to a chosen people. Such revelation is the result of the sovereign's purpose to make himself known.

The Strong One

In antiquity an extensively used term for deity was the word *El* and its related forms: *Elohim*, *Elim*, and *Eloah*. *El* seems to bc related to the verbal root *ul* ("to be strong"). An alternate etymology yields the idea of commanding leadership. In fact, all variants in derivation support this sense of power or might in its most dynamic form. Isaiah sarcastically named the idols *elilim*, a diminutive of *El*, to show the impotence of the heathen deities in contrast to the true God of Israel. *Elilim* could be translated "good-for-nothing-ones."

Elohim is a masculine plural noun that we may call "the plural of greatness." It is an intensification of the singular *El*, expressing the superhuman power of the Almighty. "In the beginning *Elohim* created the heaven and the earth" (Gen. 1:1). *Elohim* signifies the "put-er forth" of power. He is the Being to whom all power belongs.

When *El* is combined with *Elyon* ("highest"), we arrive at a conception of God which elevates him above all else in the universe. *Elyon* is rooted in *elah*, which means "to go up" or "to be elevated," thus declaring the extreme exaltation of God. It is in the name of *El Elyon*, the Most High God, that Melchizedek blesses Abraham (Gen. 14:19). Notwithstanding the election of Abraham, a select few outside the patriarchal family were sovereignly introduced to the God of their salvation. Melchizedek, a man with pre-Abrahamic knowledge of God, was one of these recipients of God's grace. A profound principle is operative here. There is a chosen people called through election, which, although particularistic, extends beyond ethnic groups to encompass all whom God has sovereignly made the objects of his grace. While *El* and *Elohim* are found in Canaanite texts relating to deity, the one upon whom Melchizedek calls is the sole possessor of heaven and earth. Similarly, Abraham thinks of God as the only true creator-sustainer of the universe (Gen. 14:22).

Further affirmation of God's sovereign administration is found in the Aramaic texts of Daniel, where *'Illā'āh* and *'Elyōwnîn* (synonyms for *Elyon*) bear witness to the absolute control of God over all creation (Dan. 4:17; 7:18, 22, 25, 27). In the seventh chapter, we see how God volitionally identifies himself with a group called "saints," his "called-out ones." In concert with this, Jacob refers to God as *El-Elohe Israel* ("God is the God of Israel"), thereby attesting to the special revelation of God leading to the salvation of his elect. The adoption of Israel was not an act of choice upon the part of Israel but rather the product of a sovereign administration of grace subsumed under the word *covenant*, of which Adam was the original partaker.

Why should God have chosen a select minority as opposed to the countless cultures extant both then and now? This irresolvable mystery must be considered within the context of God's sovereignty. Job affirmed that every soul is in his hand, even "the breath of all mankind" (Job 12:10). It is God that "leads counselors away spoiled, and makes the judges fools" (v. 17). If God is the *Deus absconditus* to some, it is because he has chosen to remain incomprehensible to them.

Stability

El is intensified when combined with *Shaddai* to represent God's self-disclosure during his people's earliest history. Commonly rendered "the Almighty God," *El Shaddai* communicates the majesty, might, and stability of God.

Rabbinical tradition says the name's two particles speak of complete sufficiency. *Shaddai* is related to the verb *shadad*, which speaks of unlimited power (Isa. 13:6; Joel 1:15). The word is also related to the Aramaic for mountain, *shadu*. Thus, Ezekiel fell awestruck to the ground before the presence of *Shaddai* (Ezek. 1:24, 28). This name provided Israel with transitional knowledge leading from the use of *Elohim* to the extraordinary personal revelation of God as *Yahweh*. While *Elohim* revealed God primarily in terms of his rule over creation in general, *El Shaddai* made men aware of the way in which God subdued and molded all these forces in the performance of his will. *El Shaddai* also speaks of God as provider for his children. Thus, the ancient Jews referred to him as *Makohm* ("place"), for in him all things subsisted and were sustained. Abraham knew him as the source of life's necessities (Gen. 22:13), for he who promised was faithful. God's immutable sovereignty backed every promise. In the context of Genesis 17, God's self-presentation as *El Shaddai* served as a pledge that, despite the barrenness of Sarah's womb and the virtual impotence of Abraham, God could and would provide the innumerable progeny he had promised. "Overpowerer" would serve excellently as a synonym for this name.

God is called *Shaddai* more frequently in Job than in any other Old Testament book. Such usage is deeply meaningful for, in the midst of perplexity and anguish, cognition of the sovereignty of God becomes all the more necessary. Because he is gracious, his sufficiency is made abundantly real in our extensive insufficiencies. There is bittersweet release for the one who, in the throes of conflict, can say with Job, "The arrows of *Shaddai* are within me" (Job 6:4). Although Job's problem with suffering is never fully resolved, a vision of his Kinsman-Redeemer supplies his deepest need. The key to Job's consolation is simple trust in God, in which lies the essential redemptive theme of the book bearing his name. The fact that God has promised never to leave or forsake his children engenders trust in his sovereignty.

The second syllable in *Shaddai—ai*—is commonly a possessive suffix in the Hebrew. God's limitless ownership is a key factor in our understanding of his sovereignty.

Divine Ownership

Ownership is also an integral factor in the use of the word *Adonai* ("Lord"), another prominent word in the patriarchal period. In Genesis 24:12, 14, Abraham is addressed as such to denote his role as a master of servants. *Adonai* may actually be translated "my lord" as it expresses the user's submission to his master. The derivation of *Adonai* conveys the idea of judging and ruling, thereby pointing to God as the almighty monarch whose reign governs the inanimate as well as the animate. At the very least, it signifies God's complete ownership of each member of the human family.

The Only True Name

Yahweh, occurring some six thousand times in the Old Testament, is, strictly speaking, the only true name of God. Its spiritual usage is not found in the history of Semitic tribes contemporaneous with ancient Israel. While other Old Testament designations describe his dealings and attributes, *Yahweh* is what Genesis calls *the* name of God. The name occurs more than twice as much as its nearest competitor, *Elohim*.

Even before the time of Christ, Jews feared to pronounce this name, substituting Adonai whenever the four Hebrew letters representing *Yahweh* (Y-H-W-H, called the *Tetragrammaton*) appeared in Scripture. By so doing they hoped to avoid the penalty they found in their lamentable misreading of Leviticus 24:16—"He that blasphemes the name of [Yahweh], he shall surely be put to death." Students of the apocryphal literature notice the conspicuous absence of that divine name there. Among orthodox Jews, there has always been the belief that the Messiah would have the right and ability to restore the lost pronunciation. "Jehovah" is certainly inaccurate.

It is with the call of Moses that this name takes on special significance. It is explained in Exodus 3:14 as "I AM THAT I AM" or, better, "I will be what I will be." Intrinsically, the name displays God's continual presence and the demonstration of his power to redeem his people. It points to his constancy as the covenant-keeping Redeemer. Hence we read, "I am [Yahweh], I change not" (Mal. 3:6). By using the name with Moses, God was making known the fact that he would bless Moses and his people as he had blessed the patriarchs before him. In all this Yahweh shows self-determination; he is not influenced by outside forces. Shem's inspired note of praise in Genesis 9:26 affirms this fact. In effect the patriarch said, "Blessed be *Yahweh*, because he is willing to be the God of Shem."

The redemptive value of the name became experientially revealed to the enslaved Israelites in Egypt in a way previously unknown (Exod. 6:3). Moreover, that miraculous deliverance showed God's sovereign rulership over all the forces of nature, including the false Egyptian gods. The positive determinism of Yahweh's revelation is forcefully stated when he says, "I will take you to me for a people, and I will be to you a God: and you shall know that I am [*Yahweh*] your God" (Exod. 6:7). What could more fittingly portray God's sovereignty than that trio of expressions: "I will take," "I will be," and "you shall know"? The serpent of Genesis knows nothing of Yahweh's sovereign redeeming strength and refers to God only with the general word *Elohim*.

Yahweh's words "[I] will be gracious to whom I will be gracious" (Exod. 33:19) are intimately related to the definition provided by Exodus 3:14. These words will always be a source of deepest joy to God's elect, for he cannot be thwarted in carrying them out.

The psalmists are prolific in regard to this theme. In Psalm 23, in a type of biblical shorthand, David records the sevenfold operation of God's redemptive power in his life: Yahweh makes, leads, restores, guides, is with him, prepares a table, anoints. "To know him" in the sense of Exodus 6:7 implies a practical experimental penetration into his sovereignty. Genesis 15:6 says literally that Abraham "developed trust in *Yahweh.*" But what motivated that trust? Was it not the sure word of the sovereign God in concert with the direct revelation of Yahweh to Abraham? It is the same today as it was in the time of Elijah when the word of Yahweh assured the salvation of seven thousand souls

(1 Kings 19:18). Your salvation and mine is determined by the one who exercises the right to make one vessel unto honor and another unto dishonor.

The title Adonai Yahweh occurs 293 times in the Old Testament, 217 of them in the book of Ezekiel, where the prevalent theme is the sovereignty of God. Ezekiel concludes logically that men should glorify God. It was in the midst of spiritual decline and lethargy that Ezekiel proclaimed that message. His exalted vision rested on the formula *co-amar Adonai Yahweh* ("Thus says the Lord *Yahweh*" [Ezek. 2:4]). We of this generation must, as Ezekiel, see God's commands as preemptory and irresistible. "As Yahweh spoke, so he also did" is the recurrent witness of Scripture and history (Gen. 21:1; Ezek. 17:24).

To the serpent God said, "I will put enmity between you and the woman, and between your seed and her seed" (Gen. 3:15). Here was no act requiring or even soliciting cooperative assistance. God did not say to Adam and Eve, "Be at enmity with the serpent," but "I will put enmity . . ." The entire revelation attests to the manner in which that enmity was sovereignly established. That God should manifest himself as man's Savior reveals an entirely autonomous act, for man has nothing within him entitling him to such favor from God. The imposition of the covenant of grace upon man stems from a purely one-sided movement of which God is the sole initiator.

Lord of Hosts

Yahweh is often linked with *Tzebaoth*, which shows God as commander omnipotent in the universe. In the east, the might of a king is measured by the splendor of his retinue. *Yahweh's* hosts include all created agencies and beings. Isaiah records God's complete mastery of creation, beginning at Isaiah 24:23, where even the glory of the sun is but an adumbration of his glory. The absolutely exhaustive control of *Yahweh Tzebaoth* motivated the translators of the Septuagint to render the name *ho Pantokrator* ("the all-ruler"). In 1 Samuel 1:11, Hannah's prayer to *Yahweh Tzebaoth* appropriately reflects humble submissiveness in cognition of God's sovereignty. Indeed, apart from such cognition, all prayer is reduced to little more than wishful thinking. *Yahweh Tzebaoth* occurs most frequently following the Babylonian exile, some eighty citations given in Jeremiah alone. The postexilic usage evinces the warlike quality of the name and reaffirms the invincibility of the Sovereign who liberates Israel. In conjunction with this militant picture, we observe that the Messiah himself is prepared for combat, as seen in Isaiah 11:5. In the midst of brilliant visions of the end time, Isaiah sees Christ as a warrior.

Consonant with this vision are his preincarnate manifestations as the Angel of Yahweh, also revealed as "the angel of his presence" (Isa. 63:9; see also Gen. 16:7; 22:15–16; Exod. 3:2–4). Once again, it is God who sovereignly takes the initiative, invading man's space-time continuum that a fallen race may have access to life, and that more abundantly. The paradox of the Angel, who is both identified with the Lord (Gen. 22:11–12) and yet distinguishable from him (Gen. 22:15–16), remains enigmatic until the God-Man himself appears in the fullness of time.

It is the omnipresence of *Yahweh Shammah* ("the Lord is there") that brings God's promise to fruition. The ancient hieroglyphic for God was an eye upon a scepter, to illustrate that he sees and controls all things. Many err in thinking that because God is designated as a Spirit (*Ruach*) he is without substance; for, rather than connoting immaterialness, "Spirit" actually describes the nature of the power residing in God. While God's presence may in one sense be localized, there is, nevertheless, no place in the universe where his presence is not manifested or his power lacking.

God with Us

We cannot think of the localization of that power without thinking of the Messiah, in whom God's sovereignty appears so gloriously. Despite the infrequency of *Mashiach* ("anointed") as an actual name of God, the title nonetheless points to the ideal sovereign kingship in an eschatological ruler. This potentate is the Son of God.

While the Old Testament has no single word to express the omnipotence of God, the series of descriptions pertaining to *Immanuel* ("God with us" [Isa. 7:14]) in Isaiah 9:6 certainly gives that concept full breadth. Isaiah calls him *Pele Yoetz* ("Wonderful Counselor"), *El Gibbor* ("mighty God"), *Abhi Ad* ("everlasting Father"), and *Sar Shalom* ("Prince of Peace"). The crying need of man is to know this one who, by his very nature, is a "wonder." His ministry is unique in its comprehensiveness: Prophet (Deut. 18:15ff), Priest (Ps. 110:4), King (Isa. 11:1ff.). His omniscience as Counselor (*Yoetz*) makes him the source of all truth; in fact, he is its actual embodiment. His underived existence as our paternal Christ brings inexhaustible fullness to our souls. Plenitude of life stems from the peace that passes all understanding, peace that he alone can give. Jesus spoke the words *ego eimi* ("I am") in John 8:58, thereby showing his inalienable right to the sacred name. He wields the same sword of authority as does the Father. To proclaim the sovereignty of Yahweh is also to proclaim him who said, "All authority is given unto me in heaven and in earth" (Matt. 28:18).

Would that all men knew Jesus as he is: *Yahweh Tzidkenu*, the sovereign provider of our justification (Jer. 23:6). Would that all might echo the words of the psalmist, who said, "O come, let us worship and bow down: let us kneel before the LORD our maker" (Ps. 95:6).

5

On Knowing God

J. I. PACKER

KNOWING GOD! Is there any greater theme that we could study? I hardly think so. To know God is the promise of the gospel. To know God is the supreme gift of grace. Jeremiah, looking forward to what God was going to do, spoke in these terms: "Behold, the days come, says the LORD, that I will make a new covenant with the house of Israel" (Jer. 31:31). And, according to the prophet, the consequence will be this: "They shall teach no more every man his neighbor, and every man his brother, saying, Know the LORD; for they shall all know me, from the least of them unto the greatest of them" (v. 34). That is the glory of the new covenant.

Jesus Christ came as a preacher of eternal life. On one occasion, in prayer to his Father, he defined eternal life. "This is life eternal," he said, "that they might know you the only true God, and Jesus Christ, whom you have sent" (John 17:3). The apostle John, the beloved disciple who perhaps saw deeper into Jesus's heart of love than anyone, sums up at the end of his first letter what Christ had brought to him and his fellow believers:

"We know that the Son of God is come, and has given us an understanding, that we may know him that is true" (1 John 5:20).

It is a glorious reality to know God. This is what we were made for; this is what we have been redeemed for. This is the sum of the Christian's ambition and hope. The apostle Paul assures us of this when he tells of his own hope: "That I may know him" (Phil. 3:10). In 1 Corinthians 13:12, he sums up the hope to which he looks forward: "Now I know in part; but then shall I know even as also I am known." His ambition and his hope are summed up in terms of the knowledge of God. It is man's highest dignity to know God; it is man's final fulfillment to know God. There is, I repeat, no more vital subject any of us can ever study than knowing God according to the Scriptures.

In Reformed theology, knowing God has always been a key concept. In fact, the first and best of the Reformed expositors of this theme was John Calvin himself. Calvin's *Institutes*, that basic text for the whole Reformed tradition, went through five editions from 1536 to 1559. Part of the reason for its growth from the little pocket book in 1536 to the big folio in 1559 was the developing theme of knowing God. Though it was dealt with sketchily in the first edition, and dismissed in scarcely more than a sentence, it eventually came to dominate the whole structure. The opening sentence of the 1536 *Institutes* was this: "The sum of sacred doctrine is contained in these two parts: the knowledge of God and of ourselves." In the second edition that sentence was changed into this: "The sum of our wisdom is contained in our knowledge of God and of ourselves." In the fourth edition that sentence was expanded in separate chapters, one on the knowledge of God and one on the knowledge of ourselves. Those chapters were further expanded in the final edition. In the final version, Calvin's material was arranged in four distinct books. The first book was called *Of the Knowledge of God the Creator*. The second book was called *Of the Knowledge of Christ the Redeemer*. The theme of knowing God expanded to dominate the whole work.

The full title of Calvin's *Institutes* is not *Institutio Christianae Theologiae*, which would be translated as "Basic Instruction in Christian Theology," but *Institutio Christianae Religionis*, "Basic Instruction in the Christian Religion," which is more than theology. And the knowing of God is more than theology. Knowing God is not simply cultivating true notions about God; knowing God is the practice of the Christian religion, the practice of godliness. It is in truth the basic biblical concept (and the basic Reformed concept) that sums up the life that the Christian gospel proclaims.

Let us focus on this concept and try to define it. I take all my points from Calvin.

Not Awareness Only

First, knowledge of God is more than the natural man's awareness of God. Calvin has a different phrase for that. He calls it *notitia dei* ("awareness of God") rather than *cognitio dei*, which is his regular phrase for "knowledge of God." Calvin is very emphatic that the natural man is aware of God and, try as he might, cannot get rid of this awareness. He speaks of the sense of deity, the impression of God, the conviction about God, the seed of religion that is planted in the human heart and that the natural man cannot eliminate. The natural man wishes to pretend that there is no God, but pretense it remains, because deep down he knows that God exists. Nonetheless, this awareness of God that the natural man has is not to be equated with the knowledge of God that the Christian has. To Calvin, knowledge of God is knowledge within a covenanted relationship.

Knowledge of a covenant God who has given himself to us as our God is basic to Calvin's understanding. Knowledge of God means knowledge of God as the one who has given himself to us. "Religion," said Luther, "is a matter of personal pronouns, I being able to say to God, 'My God,' and I knowing that God says to me, 'My child.'" It is in that relationship that knowledge of God becomes a reality.

Second, knowledge of God is more than any particular experience of God. For, like the biblical writers, Calvin comes out of an era when people were less self-absorbed than we are. They were more interested in the realities that they experienced than in their experiences of those realities. (When I say "experience," I mean "feeling" or "reaction to something.") It is rather difficult, I think, for us twentieth-century men to understand this distinction. We are self-absorbed. We are interested in experiences for their own sake. We are inclined to jump to the conclusion that the more intense any experience is, the more of God there must be in it. But by Bible standards, this is not so at all. Not even a conversion experience may be equated with the knowledge of God. "For," says Calvin (and the Scripture before him), "we know God by faith." Faith is an outgoing of the heart in trust. Experiences *flow* from faith, but it is a relationship of trust and not in itself an experience. Without faith there would be no conversion experience. Without faith there would be no Christian experience at all. But faith is something distinct from the experience. Faith is the outgoing of the heart to the God and Christ who are there giving themselves to us and saying, "Come, put your trust in the Father and the Son."

Third, knowledge of God is more than knowing *about* God, although knowing about God is its foundation. There is a difference between knowledge by description, in which you simply know *about* something, and knowledge by acquaintance, in which you are in direct contact with that reality.

The knowledge of God is by acquaintance, which is more than knowledge by description.

Calvin is very emphatic about what must be known about God. In the first chapter of the first edition of the *Institutes*, Calvin wrote that there are four things that must be known about God. First, God is "infinite wisdom, righteousness, goodness, mercy, truth, power and life, so that there is no other wisdom, righteousness, goodness, mercy, truth, power and life save in him." Second, "all things, both in heaven and earth were created to his glory." Third, "he is a righteous judge who sternly punishes those who swerve from his laws and do not wholly fulfill his will." And fourth, "he is mercy and gentleness, receiving kindly the rich and the poor who flee to his clemency and entrust themselves to his faithfulness." These are the four basics that we must know about God if ever we are to come to know him. But, says Calvin, to know these things and to have these things clear in our minds is not yet to know God. For knowledge of God, *cognitio dei*, is relational knowledge, knowledge that comes to us in the relation of commitment and trust, faith and reliance.

My fourth point is paradoxical, but you will see what I mean. Knowing God is, in fact, more than knowing God. For it is not knowing God in isolation; it is knowing God in his relationship to us, that relationship in which he gives himself and his gifts to us for our enrichment. In other words, knowledge of God takes place only where there is knowledge of ourselves and our need and thankful reception of God's gifts to meet our need. Calvin is so right. The knowledge of God and of ourselves—these two things together—make the sum of our wisdom. In fact, one does not begin to know God until one knows God's gracious gift offered to him in his own weakness, sin, and wretchedness; then and only then does one know God's grace.

We can now speak specifically about what is involved in knowing God. When we know God, we *apprehend* what he is, we *apply* to ourselves what he is and what he gives, and we *adore* him, the giver.

Let Calvin say this to us in his own terms: "The knowledge of God, as I understand it, is that by which we not only conceive that there is a God but also grasp what befits us and is proper to his glory, in fine, what is to our advantage to know of him. Indeed we shall not say that, properly speaking, God is known where there is no religion or piety."[1] This is the response of adoration and worship, both by lip and by heart and in life. Again Calvin says this: "We are called to a knowledge of God: not that knowledge which, content with empty speculation, merely flits in the brain."[2] It is not, in other words, just a matter of ideas. But it is a knowledge that, if we rightly grasp it and allow it to take root in our hearts, will be solid and fruitful. When Calvin says "fruitful," he means "life-changing." So true knowledge of God means bringing forth the fruit of Christlikeness. Again he says: "The knowledge of God does not rest in cold speculation but carries with it the honoring of him."[3]

Communication

So, this is what knowing God meant to Calvin and what it has meant to all Reformed theologians and what it means, I am persuaded, in the Scriptures. But how does this knowledge of God come about? What are our means of knowing God?

The usual Reformed formula—indeed, the usual Christian formula—is that knowledge of God depends upon God's revelation of himself to us. Knowledge and revelation are correlative.

1. John Calvin, *Institutes of the Christian Religion*, ed. John T. McNeill and trans. Ford Lewis Battles (Philadelphia: The Westminster Press, 1960), 39.
2. Calvin, 61.
3. Calvin, 116–17.

And that is right. Calvin insisted on it, and Reformed theologians insist on it as strongly as any Christians have ever insisted on it. Yet I sometimes find myself wishing that in place of that word *revelation*, we could substitute another word that I think would express more in modern discussion and debate. In place of *revelation*, I would like to say *communication*. The word *revelation* suggests to modern minds little more than a general display, a general exhibition of something. I believe it is very important when we think of the revelation of God always to keep in view that it is personal communication from the Creator to his creatures. That word *communication* seems to me to carry all the right vibrations and to convey all the right thoughts.

What does communication suggest? It suggests a person who approaches us, comes close to us, speaks to us, tells us about himself, opens his mind to us, gives us what he has, reveals what he knows, asks for our attention, asks for our response to what he is saying. This is the word we need in order to make clear how the knowledge of God comes to us. It comes to us through divine communication; God comes to us and makes himself known.

At this point there is a specific problem. God made us in order that he might communicate himself to us and thus draw us into loving fellowship with himself. But man has turned away from God; sin has come in; human nature has become twisted. Man is now anti-God in his basic attitudes. He is not interested in fellowship with God. It is no longer in his nature to love God; it is no longer in his nature to respond to God. He has his back to God. Because of the fall, it is now human nature to do over and over what Adam and Eve did in Genesis 3. It is our nature to treat ourselves as though we were God. We live for ourselves; we seek to bend everything to our own interest. In doing so we fight God; that is, we fight the real God. We say no to him. We push him away from the center of our life to its circumference.

So God's communication to sinful man must do more than simply present truth to his mind. It has to work in him to change his heart and his nature.

There is, says Calvin, a general communication, or "general revelation," of God to men through nature (the created order all of us are in contact with every day of our lives). In our own nature, too, there is a revelation, a communication from God. It reaches us in the same way that an awareness of light reaches us. It is immediate, inescapable, undeniable. But fallen man denies it nevertheless and turns the light that is in him into darkness.

Calvin speaks very strongly about this. He says that God has so revealed himself "in the whole workmanship of this world" that "men cannot open their eyes without being compelled to see him."[4] "This skillful ordering of the universe is for us a sort of mirror in which we may contemplate God, who is otherwise invisible."[5] "The universe . . . was founded as a spectacle of God's glory."[6] Again, Calvin calls it "a dazzling theater" of God's glory.[7] "The Lord represents both himself and his everlasting kingdom in the mirror of his works."[8]

The awareness of the Creator comes through in all our commerce with his creatures, in all our knowledge and awareness of ourselves, our identity, the workings of our conscience, and the thoughts of our own hearts. But man denies this awareness and turns it into darkness and superstition. So the world, for all its wisdom, does not know God, though this general communication of God through nature is a reality for every man.

4. Calvin, 52.
5. Calvin, 52–53.
6. Calvin, 58.
7. Calvin, 61.
8. Calvin, 63.

Three Stages

What, then, is there to do? Well, God has added to this general communication of himself in the natural order a special communication of himself in grace, in which there are three stages. Stage one is *redemption in history*. By words and works God makes himself known on the stage of history in saving action. The words are basic, for first God tells men what he is going to do. He makes the announcement, then he acts, fulfilling his word. That is how he proceeded at the Exodus when he saved Israel out of captivity in Egypt. That is what he did when in the fullness of time he sent his own Son, born of a woman, to redeem those who were under the law. He sent Christ to sinners like you and me, that we might receive the adoption of sons and so become children in his family.

Stage two is *revelation in writing*, which is the work of God inspiring the Holy Scriptures. God caused interpretive records to be written of what he had said and done, so that all men in all generations might know him and through this knowledge might come into the enjoyment of the redemptive revelation that he had made. The written record is our Bible.

The third stage in the communicative process is *reception by individuals* of the realities of redemption declared in the Scriptures. This reception becomes a reality through the work of the Holy Spirit. The Holy Spirit opens hearts to give the Word entrance and renews hearts so that we might turn around again to face God. We become new creatures in Christ. When the New Testament speaks of God revealing himself to men, it is this third stage in the process of divine communication that is normally in view, as when Jesus said, "Neither knows any man the Father, save the Son, and he to whomsoever the Son will reveal him" (Matt. 11:27), or as when Jesus said again, "Blessed are you, Simon Barjona: for flesh and blood have not revealed it unto you, but my Father who is in heaven" (Matt. 16:17). Paul uses the word *reveal* in the same way when he says that "it pleased God . . . to reveal his Son in me" (Gal. 1:15, 16). The same thought is expressed by Paul in other words when he says in 2 Corinthians 4:6 that "God, who commanded the light to shine out of darkness, has shined in our hearts, to give the light of the knowledge of the glory of God in the face of Jesus Christ."

Scripture Essential

Do you see now that stage two in the process, the inspiring of the Bible, is absolutely crucial? Calvin saw that. He regularly referred to the Bible as the "oracles of God." That, of course, is a scriptural phrase. It is Paul's phrase in Romans 3:2. Calvin took it and used it again and again to express the thought that what we have in Scripture is God's own witness to his work of salvation. Calvin observed that the Bible has a double function in relation to us sin-blinded sinners. It functions as our "schoolmaster," teaching us the truth and operating as the rule of our teaching and speaking. And it serves as our "spectacles" as well.

Calvin's illustration of spectacles speaks to me because I am nearsighted. I take off my glasses, and I cannot see people or things in front of me. I can see a sort of smudge. That is all. Calvin, who himself was nearsighted, says in effect that the natural man without the Scriptures has no more than a smudgy awareness that there is a something or a someone, but he does not know who the something or the someone is. He has just this smudgy awareness. But, says Calvin, when a nearsighted man is able to put on glasses, then he sees clearly what he saw before as only a smudge. So when we begin to study the Scriptures we begin to see clearly that person of whom before we had that unwelcome awareness. The Scriptures come to us as glasses, enabling us to focus that awareness of God and showing us precisely who and what this God is. The Scriptures are our lifeline. They alone can guide us out of the labyrinth of ignorance.

Calvin opposed any form of theology that sought to run apart from the Scriptures. He denounced it as speculation. He considered it ungodly. Consequently, he summons us to that humility which acknowledges need and is willing to be taught.

Much theology today is speculative in the sense that Calvin condemned. It patronizes the Scriptures; it stands above the Scriptures, going beyond and away from them. And it is trash, says Calvin. As one whose profession obliges him to spend a great deal of his time reading speculative theology, I can only endorse that opinion. Theology that flies away from the Scripture is trash, and one of the miseries of the modern church is that much of its books, preaching, and thinking is so much trash at this point.

What is called for now, as in Calvin's day, is the humility that bows before the Scriptures and accepts them as instruction from God. They are God preaching, God talking, God telling, God setting before us the right way to think and to talk concerning him. They are God showing us himself, God communicating to us who he is and what he has done so that we in the response of faith may truly know him and live our lives in fellowship with him.

Give Me That Book

Often Reformed people think of the Scriptures simply as a stick with which to beat unorthodoxy. When we use the phrase *biblical authority*, this is often all that we have in mind. But I want to ask this: Do you recognize the place the Bible has in God's communication of himself to you? Do you thank God for the Bible as one of his greatest gifts of grace to you? Do you recognize that it is as great and as glorious as the gift of his Son to you? It is. For if you did not have the Bible to lead you to the Son, you could never know the Son as your Savior and could never come to know God as your Father. Think of the Bible first and foremost as a gift of the grace of God and prize it accordingly.

Let us learn this from one who (quite mistakenly) went on calling himself an Arminian, when he was only a muddled Calvinist—John Wesley. Here is how Wesley expressed it in his preface to the published edition of his sermons:

> I am a creature of a day, passing through life as an arrow through the air . . . till, a few moments hence . . . I drop into an unchangeable eternity! I want to know one thing,—the way to heaven. . . . God Himself has condescended to teach the way. . . . He hath written it down in a book. O give me that book! At any price, give me the book of God! I have it: Here is knowledge enough for me. . . . I sit down alone: Only God is here. In his presence I open, I read his book; for this end, to find the way to heaven. Is there a doubt . . . ? I lift up my heart to the Father of Lights:—"Lord, . . . let me know thy will."[9]

Do you identify with that? Do you identify with John Wesley and his attitude to his Bible as a supreme gift of God's grace? I hope we all do. This Word is what the world needs if ever it is to know God. Thank God for it and value and prize it.

At the coronation of the sovereign of England, the Moderator of the Church of Scotland, a good Presbyterian, presents a Bible to the reigning monarch and speaks of it as—I quote the words exactly— "the most precious thing this world affords, the

9. John Wesley, *The Works* (Grand Rapids: Zondervan Publishing House, from the authorized edition of 1872), 5:3.

most precious thing that this world knows, God's living Word." That is true. Christ and the Scriptures belong together as gifts of the grace of God. Reformed theology begins in recognition of this truth and in glad submission to the teaching of Scripture, that from it we may learn of our Savior. God help us to begin at what is the true beginning, then. God teach us to value and prize his Holy Word.

Word and Spirit

Knowing God springs from God's communication to us. He approaches, he speaks, he shares, he summons, he calls, he gives. We by faith respond to his approach. Thus we come to know him. It is the same pattern as in any other-personal relationship.

But it is through the Holy Spirit that God gives us the Bible and through the Spirit that he brings us to acknowledge it as God's Word, to understand its message, and to respond to it in faith. It was because of his emphasis on these things that Calvin was hailed by B. B. Warfield as the "theologian of the Holy Spirit," just as, according to Warfield, Augustine should be acknowledged as the "theologian of sin" and Luther as the "theologian of justification." It was Calvin who first traced out in full what God himself tells us of the work of the Holy Spirit in announcing and applying the message of redemption. We may study it in five areas: inspiration, interpretation, authentication of Holy Scripture, biblical authority, and faith in Scripture.

Inspiration

First, inspiration. Calvin has his own way of expressing the truth of biblical inspiration. It is a formula that revolves for him around the use of four significant words or phrases. Calvin speaks first of *doctrina*. That is the Latin word that means "teaching"; teaching, he says, that comes from God. This introduces his second phrase, "the mouth of God" (*os dei*). Again and again Calvin speaks of Holy Scripture as teaching that comes to us directly from the mouth of God. That is Calvin's way of expressing its divine origin and authority. "Teaching from God"—that is his basic idea.

Moreover, he confirms this by a third phrase, "dictated by the Holy Spirit." This is an image that has caused a great deal of trouble in Christian theology, for people have persistently misunderstood it as signifying that the Holy Spirit turned the human authors of the biblical books into typewriters and that in some way their human spontaneity as thinkers and writers was suppressed. But that is not what Calvin meant when he used this image. He meant that what is written in Scripture bears the same relation to the mind of God (from which it came) as a letter written by a good secretary bears to the mind of the man from whom the secretary takes it.

Calvin does not mean to imply anything whatever about the psychology of the process of inspiration. Calvin knows perfectly well, and his comments show it on every page, that the free functioning of the penmen's minds was not in any way diminished in consequence of their inspiration. They were themselves. This point is most clearly expressed in Calvin's comments on the Psalms.

The fourth word that Calvin uses to express his doctrine of inspiration is the word *condescension*, which means what it suggests—God coming down to our level to talk baby talk, as it were, to us who are, after all, spiritual babies and who are able to understand things better that way. Calvin actually talks about God babbling in the way in which a mother will babble, talking baby talk to her child. The purpose is, says Calvin, that we may understand. God in his mercy prattles to us; he comes down to our level, puts things in a simple, unpolished way, sometimes in a way that may be crude and harsh. But we understand it better that way. The Scriptures speak in a much simpler way than most theologians do. That is a fact. "This is God's mercy," says Calvin. God speaks in a simple manner so that we his children will understand. I think that many simple Christians would find the *Institutes* too hard for them. Yet the things that Calvin spells out with unrivaled precision are in the Scriptures put in a simpler and less guarded form, and simple Christian souls do not misunderstand these things when they meet them in the Word of God.

It is part of Calvin's wisdom to have spoken in these terms and not to have ducked the issue of acknowledging the condescension of God in the inspiring of Scripture. The modern error about the Bible has been to say that because it is so obviously and completely human it cannot be 100 percent divine. I say, Nonsense! No Christian will argue in that way about the person of the Lord Jesus Christ, who was also 100 percent human. How absurd, then, to suppose that this is the right way to argue about the Scriptures!

Modern skeptical theology has gone on to say, "But surely it is not possible to believe that the whole Bible is true, that everything that the biblical writers intend to assert in God's name is, in truth, his *doctrina*." But Calvin does say that. Calvin was insistent that the Bible is all true. He was one of the clearest exponents of the thought of biblical inerrancy that the church has seen.

Interpretation

Second, what has Calvin to say about the interpretation of Holy Scripture? He says that because Scripture is 100 percent human, the only right way to interpret it must be to follow what

God's human spokesmen expressed. The way into the mind of God the Holy Spirit is through the mind of the human author. If you cut your interpretation loose from the human author and allegorize without regard to what he meant, you are not developing a super-spiritual exposition of Scripture, you are only falling into an extremely perverse misinterpretation.

But because Scripture is also 100 percent divine and all of it is truth from God, you must expound Scripture coherently. That is, you must allow one passage to throw light on another and refuse to set one passage against another, because it all comes from the mind of God and God will not contradict himself. Furthermore, said Calvin, because Scripture is bearing witness to the comprehensive purpose of God, namely, to glorify himself through Jesus Christ, we must understand that Jesus Christ is the reference point for all that Scripture says. Calvin expressed this by saying that Christ is the *scopus*, that is to say, the reference point throughout the whole Bible. And, says Calvin, you have not understood any part of Scripture adequately until you have related it to God's purpose in Christ.

Successful biblical interpretation will not be achieved in our own strength. We must invoke God the Spirit as our teacher and ask him to give us light on the meaning and message of the textbook he inspired. Without his help we shall only misunderstand and go astray.

Authentication

The third topic is the authentication of Holy Scripture. How do we know that the Bible is the Word of God? It is not sufficient, says Calvin, to appeal to the fact that the great part of the Christian church down the centuries has been convinced that it is. Though that is true, nonetheless the church is only a human witness. Our conviction of the divinity of the Scripture must be based on more than human witness. Only the Holy Spirit himself can convince us that this book is like no other book, that it is divine. The parallel here is the way in which the Holy Spirit, witnessing with and through the gospel, makes the deity of the Lord Jesus Christ self-evidencing to those who believe in him.

Do you find within yourself the possibility of denying the divinity of Jesus Christ? Do you find it a possibility within yourself to doubt or deny the divinity of the Scriptures? If your honest answer before God is no, then bless his name. What has happened is that you have benefited from the witness of the Holy Spirit, who has made you aware of the deity of the Living Word and the authority of the written Word. This, said Calvin, is how all Christians come to know that the Bible is indeed the Word of God. The Spirit makes them so aware of its divine quality and power that they do not find themselves able to doubt it.

Authority

And what about the authority of the Scriptures? Calvin's conviction that the Scriptures must be the rule of our speaking and thinking is illustrated most vividly by what he has to say about the Anabaptists, on the one hand, and the Roman Catholics, on the other. The Anabaptists of Calvin's day were similar to the liberal and radical theologians of our time, for they appealed to the spirit in their own minds rather than what was said in the Scriptures. They said, "Because we have spiritual intuitions that come strong upon us, we are going to follow them. We accept them as from the Spirit of God; if this means leaving the Bible behind, well, so much the worse for the Bible." Calvin denied this, for he denied that the Spirit contradicts himself. Do you think that the spirit in your hearts is the Spirit of God when that spirit is speaking contrary to what the Spirit of God says in the Scriptures? Then do you not see, asks Calvin, that you are being led by false fire?

Calvin also argued against the Roman Catholics who allegorized away the plain meaning of Scripture. This is your trouble, said Calvin: You do not take the God-given Word seriously. So how can we relate, how can I help you, how can we talk together about the things of God when you will not take the Scriptures seriously? This issue still has to be pressed in order to clear up the theological confusions of our time.

Faith in the Scriptures

Finally, a word about faith in our Scriptures. The Christian, says Calvin, is the man who trembles at the Word of God. The true Christian is captive to what God has said in all his thinking, believing, and living. The true Christian lives by the promise of God, by the promise of mercy in Christ. This is his hope. The true Christian lives by the command of God. He gives his life to the Lord in obedience; both the promises he clings to and the commands he obeys are found in the Word of God. So it is to the Scriptures that he cleaves and by the Scriptures that he lives. In response to God's communication, he lives in the communion with God that those who have faith in God's Word, who respond to God's utterance, truly know. This, says Calvin, is his knowledge of God, and this is eternal life.

Did Calvin have it right? I believe he did. This is the clear teaching of Paul in 2 Timothy 3:16: "All scripture is [breathed out of God], and is profitable for doctrine, for reproof, for correction, for instruction in righteousness." Yes, Calvin had it right. And may God help us to hold fast to the truth of biblical inspiration and authority taught so vividly by Calvin and brought home so strongly by the Spirit to the hearts of all God's people.

You and I, as Reformed Christians, are probably nodding our heads. We are saying, "Yes, yes, this is not unfamiliar and, of course, it's very true and very important, and it's good to hear it again. Yes, fine." But how seriously do you take it yourself? How much are you prepared to let God tell you about himself and about yourself from the written Word? Are you prepared to let God tell you humbling things from the Scriptures? Are you prepared to let God convict you of sin and bring you low? The test of whether we really accept the Reformed understanding of divine communication through the Scriptures is whether you and I are open to the Scriptures and day by day are learning from the Scriptures. Let every one of us examine himself. It is not enough to be correct in our beliefs about the Scriptures if God is not day by day dealing with us through the Scriptures.

Thus it is that the Spirit through the Word communicates with us as from the Lord, and so it is, and only so, that our knowledge of God deepens and grows and becomes the rich reality of eternal life that God made it to be.

6

Why We Do Not Know God

R.C. SPROUL

IN ORDER to speak to the question "Why don't we know God?" we must first grant that we do, in a sense, know God. So we can hardly speak to the question "Why don't we?" without making the kind of distinction that Dr. Packer makes. Dr. Packer distinguishes between the different ways in which we may know God. He speaks of the distinction between *notitia* and cognitio—that is, the difference between an intellectual awareness or mental apprehension of something and a more profound or deep relational knowledge of someone or something.

Obviously, the Bible uses the verb "to know" in at least these two ways and perhaps even more widely. There are different levels, degrees, or ways in which we can know things and persons. That is why the Scriptures say on some occasions that men do not know God, that men are in darkness concerning God, yet on other occasions that men do know God. Unless the Bible is speaking with a forked tongue, or unless we violate radically the Reformed principle of the coherency of Scripture, we have to conclude that the Bible is speaking from different perspectives about different kinds of knowledge. Perhaps we can circumvent the dilemma by making these distinctions.

But one thing is certain: no one knows God at the depth to which it is possible to know him. And that is the question with which we must wrestle: Why do we not know God as intimately, deeply, personally, and comprehensively as it is possible for us to know him?

Willful Ignorance

The answer to that question does not require an extended dissertation. The reason that we do not know God as intimately, deeply, personally, and comprehensively as we possibly could is because *we do not want to know God* intimately, deeply, and comprehensively. Moreover, even though we may be redeemed, even though we may be "the elite of the elect," there still remains within us the residual elements of our fallenness. Our natures have been regenerated, but the sin that dwells within us has not been eradicated and will not be, this side of glory. So as long as there remains any disposition within us to sin, there is a propensity toward ignorance of the things of God.

I would like to focus our attention on a detailed analysis of why men do not know God to the degree that it is possible to know him. The basis for this analysis is Romans 1, beginning at verse 18.

In the part of the prologue that is found in Romans 1:16–18, Paul maintains that he is not ashamed of the gospel, for it is the power of God for salvation to everyone who has faith. Then we find the thematic statement of the epistle: "For [in the gospel] is the righteousness of God revealed from faith to faith:

as it is written, The just shall live by faith" (v. 17). This is the topic sentence for the whole epistle: the righteousness of God is revealed through faith. So, in a word, Paul is concerned with revelation. But notice, he begins in verse 18 not with the revelation of God's mercy, grace, or justification but with the revelation of God's wrath: "For the wrath of God is revealed from heaven against all ungodliness and unrighteousness of men" (v. 18).

What we find here, as always in Scripture, is that God's wrath is never arbitrary, capricious, irrational, or demonic, but that it is always a response to something evil. God's wrath is revealed against unrighteousness and ungodliness. It is not a wrath revealed against righteousness, godliness, or piety but against unrighteousness and ungodliness. *Unrighteousness* and *ungodliness* are general terms—wide-sweeping, wide-encompassing descriptive terms. But we must not stop here, for Paul moves from the general to the particular. He does not leave us to wonder about what particular form of unrighteousness, what specific kind of ungodliness is provoking the wrath of God. Rather, Paul names the child. He mentions it in the second clause of the sentence: "For the wrath of God is revealed from heaven against all ungodliness and unrighteousness of men, who hold [that is, 'suppress'] the truth in unrighteousness." The specific provocation of God's wrath is human suppression of truth.

The old King James Version's phrase "hold the truth in unrighteousness" seems a bit archaic, does it not? How does one hold truth? Truth is an abstract thing; truth is not quantitative. How can we use tactile, empirical terms to describe truth? We do not hold truth; we hold a wristwatch, or we hold on to something. But there are different ways to hold things. If I hold a wristwatch, that is one kind of holding. If I hold on to a lectern, that is another kind of holding. If I hold my wife, hopefully that is an altogether different kind of holding. What kind of holding does the apostle have in mind here? Well, notice that we can hold something up, or we can hold something down. The verb used here literally means "to hold down, to incarcerate, to hold back," and it suggests the notion that one must use force to repress a counterforce. The way I like to think of "holding down" is of a giant spring compressed to its point of highest tension. In order to hold that spring in place, one must exert all kinds of counterpressure to keep it compressed; otherwise it will spring up by its own tension and perhaps even injure the one who is seeking to hold it back.

So why is Paul using this verb with respect to truth? He is talking about the human effort that brings the wrath of God upon man. It is man's active, positive resistance to God's truth.

Sufficient Revelation

The reason that God is angry is further elucidated in Romans 1:19, where Paul says, "Because that which may be known of God is manifest in them; for God has shown it unto them." If Paul had merely said, "What could have been known about God was available to man," that would have been reason enough for God to reveal his wrath against those who did not avail themselves of a divinely given opportunity to know him. That in itself would have been a serious sin against our Creator. But Paul is not simply saying God has made knowledge of himself available to men and men have never made use of this opportunity. No, he is saying that the knowledge of God that he has revealed to all men has been made plain, not obscure, and that mankind has *rejected* it.

Let me comment on that with an illustration from the academic world. There are different ways in which you can bring students to a state of knowledge. You can say to them, "Look, we have a course in the doctrine of God. I am the professor in this course, but I am not going to teach you anything; I am simply going to moderate the course. Each student is responsible to lecture. If you want to know about the doctrine of God, just go to the library and find those books that have something to say about the doctrine of God and then come in and give your paper." That is one way I could do it. Or I could say, "Look, I want you to do heavy research about the doctrine of God. So I am going to take all the books in the library that deal with the doctrine of God and put them together in one place on the reserve shelf. I am going to make it easy for you to discover this information." In other words, I would be facilitating the student's efforts to learn something about the doctrine of God. Or, finally, I could go even further. I could put those books on the reserve shelf, and then I could take the student by the hand, march him over to the library, show him where the reserve shelf is, take each book off the shelf, open it up to the first page, and say to him, "Listen to this," and start to read it.

I think that Paul is getting at something like this last illustration. God does not just make the knowledge available. He shows himself to us, as the apostle says. How thoroughly that knowledge has been received remains a question. But one thing is certain: God has revealed himself to all men with sufficient clarity and with sufficient content as to render men inexcusable. He has presented himself with enough clarity, with enough revelation, to remove the cry of ignorance as a justifying reason for a person's rejection of him.

Assured Results

In Romans 1:21, Paul goes on to say that when men refuse to honor God and refuse to acknowledge him even though they know he is there, their thinking becomes "foolish" and their minds "darkened." Have you ever read the works of David Hume? Have you ever read the works of Jean-Paul Sartre? These men are great thinkers. David Hume, I think, is one of the most formidable opponents that the Christian faith has ever had to wrestle with. How can men who have clearly and blatantly denied the existence of God be so scholarly and so knowledgeable and manifest such high gifts of intelligence? The answer is in this text. Once a man refuses to acknowledge what he knows to be true, he can go on to construct magnificent systems of philosophy. He can manifest gifts of intellectual acumen and brilliance. But if he is consistent, if his starting point in the procedure involves an obstinate rejection of what he knows to be true, his system can end only in futility. Imagine the scientist who starts his scientific endeavor by denying what he knows to be the basic facts. The only way such a scientist can arrive at any kind of truth is by a happy inconsistency, by compounding his errors to such a degree that possibly he will be fortunate enough to stumble onto some truth.

The pagan adds insult to injury, Paul continues, for not only does he begin his systematic approach by refusing to acknowledge what he knows to be true and thereby working continuously with a darkened mind, but, having done this, he tells the world that he is wise. Paul says, "Professing themselves to be wise, they became fools" (Rom. 1:22). Sinful man, after he repudiates what he knows to be true, then has the audacity to say to God and to the world, "I am a wise man." But God says that the wisdom of sinful man is foolishness!

In the Scriptures the designation *fool* is not primarily an intellectual evaluation. When God says that a man is a fool, he is not saying that he is dull-witted. He is not saying that he has a low IQ or that he is a poor student. The term *fool* is a judgment of man's character. It is more of a moral evaluation than an intellectual one. It is the fool who says in his heart, "There is no God."

Foolishness is in many of the catalogues of serious sins in the New Testament, along with adultery and murder and things like that. Foolishness is a moral refusal to deal honestly with truth.

Undefined Anxiety

We notice next that men's foolishness is compounded. Claiming to be wise, they became fools and exchanged "the glory of the incorruptible God" (Rom. 1:23) for images resembling mortal man, birds, animals, or reptiles. Therefore, "God also gave them up to uncleanness through the lusts of their own hearts, to dishonor their own bodies between themselves: who changed the truth of God into a lie, and worshiped and served the creature more than the Creator, who is blessed forever" (vv. 24–25).

What happens after the truth is held down, after the truth is repressed? Is there a vacuum? No! Immediately an exchange takes place. Substitution occurs.

It is valuable to talk about this in contemporary psychological terms. Johannes Spavink, the Dutch scholar, finds in this text a statement about man's psychological prejudice. Spavink asks: Why do men repress or suppress things? He says that knowledge that is most likely to be suppressed is knowledge that comes to us in the framework of the traumatic. We try to push down knowledge that frightens us or is unpleasant. We have a kind of psycho-cybernetic system with which we screen from our conscious mind those things that are unpleasant. But the question I ask you in modern psychological terms is this: Is the memory of a threatening or traumatic experience *destroyed* by our repression? I do not know of any psychologist or biochemist who would say that those memory notions or images are destroyed. Rather, we bury them or push them down.

So, our present state of consciousness is dark, but the knowledge has not been destroyed. For example, let us say that I have repressed negative feelings about my mother. I am not even conscious of these feelings. But I begin to have undefined anxiety. I begin to worry, and I do not know why I am worried. When I begin to experience restlessness, I go to a psychologist to help me work through my anxiety state. The doctor says, "What's the matter?"

I say, "I have anxiety."

"Why do you have anxiety?"

"I don't know. That's why I came to see you. I'm worried, and I don't know why I'm worried. Help me to find out."

The doctor begins to probe my inner man to see where the injury is and how I can be brought again to health and wholeness. As he goes through my medical history, he does not pay attention simply to the words I say. He is also carefully observant of my mannerisms, my gestures, and every kind of symbolic activity with which I am communicating my deepest feelings. Eventually in our discussions he notices that every time he asks me about my mother, or every time I say something about my mother, I twitch my shoulder. So he thinks, "Every time Sproul says something about his mother, he has this awful twitch." He asks, "Do you have any kind of bad feelings about your mother?"

"My mother?" *twitch* I ask in astonishment. "I don't feel anything bad about my mother!" *twitch*

But he knows that somewhere in the past I have had a bad experience with my mother, and he knows that this knowledge has not been destroyed but only exchanged for the gesture. In this way it is (perhaps) still a problem but not quite as threatening as the original experience. In the same way, most people do not say simply, "There is no God"; rather they create a new God, one who is less threatening, less terrifying, less of a problem.

Let me illustrate this. A few years ago I was watching the David Frost show, and he was interviewing Madalyn Murray O'Hair. They began discussing whether or not there is a God, and David Frost suddenly became a great champion of the Christian faith, defending it against O'Hair. The discussion got so out of hand that Frost became angry and decided to determine the controversy by a show of hands. He turned to the studio audience and asked, "How many of you believe in some kind of supreme being, some kind of higher power, something greater than yourselves?" Almost everybody in the audience raised his hand.

I waited breathlessly to see what Madalyn Murray O'Hair would say to that kind of response. She said, "Well, what do you expect from the masses who come to this studio? What do they know? Give them time to catch up with modern knowledge, and this myth will disappear." That is the tack she took. I thought that if she had been clever she would have said, "Just a minute, Mr. Frost. Let *me* pose the question." Then, turning to the audience, she would say something like this: "I know that some of you believe in something higher than yourself, some higher power, some faceless, nameless, contextless, unknown god who makes no claims on your existence, who never stands in judgment over your morality, who does not demand the sacrifice of your life. Anybody can believe in that kind of god. But do you believe in Yahweh, the Lord God of Israel, who thunders from Sinai, 'You will have no other gods before me'? Do you believe in a god who demands obedience to his perfect law and who calls men to repentance? How many of you believe in a god who makes absolute demands upon your life?" What do you suppose the vote would have been like?

The "Supreme Being," the "Ground of Being," "Ultimate Concern"—all these titles are nonthreatening. They have no substance. They represent our most sophisticated efforts at idolatry, in which we exchange the truth of God for a lie, a nonthreatening lie. They speak of a God who never judges us, who never calls us to repentance, a cosmic grandfather who says, "Boys will be boys." That is the kind of God we have, not only in the secular world but in our churches.

The Immutable God

When I was writing the book *Psychology of Atheism*, I worked through three great attributes of God: holiness, sovereignty, and omniscience. But then I remembered a sermon I had read years before by Jonathan Edwards titled "Man Naturally God's Enemy." I wondered what Edwards had to say about why men hate God. So I went back to read that sermon. At the beginning Edwards said, "There are four things about God that make men hate him." I thought, "Four things? What did I miss?" And I wondered if Edwards had found the same things I had found.

He said, "The first thing that terrifies man is God's holiness."

I said, "Aha! I got one right!"

Then he said, "The second thing man hates about God is his omniscience." By this time my opinion of Edwards as a scholar was rising.

He went on, "The third thing that men hate about God is his sovereignty." I could hardly believe that I had put my finger on the same things. But what was the fourth one? What had I missed?

I turned the page and read, "Perhaps you are wondering what the fourth one is?" Edwards had stolen the words right out of my mouth. Then I read: "The fourth thing about God that men hate is his immutability." Immutability? Why would that be so threatening? Why should that bother us? Edwards explained. "Man faces this dilemma: Not only does he know and know clearly that God is holy and omniscient and sovereign, but he knows that God will always be holy, he will always be omniscient, he will always be sovereign. And there is nothing we can possibly do to make him less holy, less omniscient, or less sovereign. These attributes are not open to negotiation. We cannot find God involved in a process of change whereby he can enter into certain mutations to compromise with us."

From age to age, the hound of heaven brings his light into a world of darkness; but men love the darkness rather than the light because their deeds are evil.

7

Why We Must Know God

R.C. SPROUL

WHY MUST we know God? I have thought of several ways to approach that question. First, I thought I would go to Acts 17 to Paul's confrontation with the philosophers of Athens, in which he tells them that in former days of ignorance God through his forbearance overlooked that ignorance but now commands all men everywhere to repent. I also thought of approaching this theme from the perspective of duty, that the reason why we must know God is that God *commands* us to know him. But one day I was reading again the account of Jesus's experience in the wilderness when he was tempted by Satan. And from that particular experience of Christ it came to me that the real answer to the question is *that we might live*. It is as simple as that. We must know God in order to live as authentic human beings.

Two Temptations

So, let us examine the New Testament account of the temptation of Jesus as recorded in Luke 4:1–13. I would like to compare and contrast the setting of that temptation with the primordial temptation of Adam and Eve in the garden of Eden.

In this brief account we have a description of the text to which Jesus Christ, the second Adam, was put by God. In order to fully understand it, we must consider the context of the temptation. We read that the Spirit of God led Jesus into the wilderness. The place of the experience of temptation is, I think, significant. In the Old Testament, the place of the temptation is paradise. But Jesus is sent into the wilderness. Adam's temptation comes in lush surroundings. He is not thrown out into the wilderness, but rather the temptation comes to him in the garden of Eden, in a place where he is surrounded with beauty, provision, comfort, and the security of knowing the nearness of the presence of God. Yet Adam, in the midst of all this, falls to the tempter.

Moreover, when Adam falls, he is not alone. But Jesus undergoes his temptation in the context of solitude, a context which demands exceptional strength, integrity, and character.

Recall the creation account, how every stage of creation is finished with a statement of benediction from God. He creates the heavens and the seas, and he looks at what he has done and says, "That is good." Where is the first place in Scripture that we hear the malediction of God? Where do we see God not making a statement of blessing upon the situation which he views? We see it when God considers the state of Adam in his loneliness and says, "It is not good that the man should be alone" (Gen. 2:18). His first malediction is on loneliness! Yet the same Spirit of God who has said in Adam's case, "It is not good that the man should be alone," drives the Son of God into the wilderness, into a state of solitude, where he has no one to speak to, no suitable helpmate to comfort him, to commune with him, or to participate with him in his ordeal.

Soren Kierkegaard has pointed out the anxiety-producing effects of what he calls "existential solitude." Man knows of no more cruel or effective punishment in the penal system of Western civilization than to consign a person to solitary confinement. It is in solitary confinement that a person's will begins to weaken and his resistance fades. He becomes uncertain, frightened, insecure. The test comes to Adam in the midst of fellowship and communion with his wife. To Christ it comes in solitude.

Jean-Paul Sartre dramatically paints the picture for us of a man seated in a cafe—and I am sure he had himself in mind, since he was known to frequent the little cafes on the left bank of Paris. The man sits in the corner, orders his coffee, minds his own business, then suddenly begins to *feel* eyes upon the back of his neck. He steals a glance behind him and notices two people looking quickly away and realizes that they have just been discussing him. Suddenly he becomes aware of himself as a person, and it is threatening, scary! If while giving a talk I should suddenly note the fact that everybody in the room was looking at me, and if I should imagine that they were making judgments about me as a person—asking, "Why does he wear his hair like that? Why doesn't he wear a suit instead of mismatched trousers and jacket? Why does he wear a checkered sports coat? Why does he make those raving and ranting gestures all the time?"—if I stopped and thought that everybody was evaluating me as a person, I would be so terrified and paralyzed from the existential self-awareness that I would not be able to speak.

But Jesus is completely alone in the wilderness. We can spiritualize this account and say, "Well, the Father is there, and the angels are there—though they are invisible." But from a human perspective Jesus is alone. What I am trying to get at is that the test that comes to Christ comes in the context of the most difficult circumstances conceivable.

Not only is Jesus alone, not only is he in the wilderness, but he is in the middle of a fast. Satan comes to Adam and Eve when, presumably, they are full from eating of the trees in the garden. And if we read between the lines of the Old Testament narrative, it seems as though it takes Satan only about five minutes to produce the fall of Adam and Eve. But in Jesus's case, Satan waits for forty days. He waits until Jesus is at the absolute edge of human endurance, when he is severely weakened by the lack of basic physical necessities.

Has God Said?

Let us turn now from the differences between the two temptations to a consideration of the ways in which they are similar.

What is the first thing Satan does when he comes to Adam and Eve in the garden? He asks the woman a question. He does not come with a direct assault against her integrity but asks, "Did God say you should not eat of any of the trees of the garden?" Of course, that is not *really* what God had said! No! God had said, "Of every tree of the garden you may freely eat: but [the sole restriction] of the tree of the knowledge of good and evil, you shall not eat of it: for in the day that you eat thereof you shall surely die" (Gen. 2:16–17). Do you think that Satan knew what God had said to Adam and Eve? I, for one, think he knew very well. Why then does he come with that kind of a question? Why does he say, "Did God say you cannot eat of any of the trees of the garden?" What comes next explains it. For notice that as soon as Eve says, "No, he said that we can eat of all the trees of the garden except this one lest we die," Satan immediately answers, "You will not die, but you will be as gods, knowing good and evil."

You will not die! What is at stake here? What is the issue? Food? Trees? Freedom? No! The thing that is in question in the temptation of Adam is the same thing that is in question in the temptation of Christ: the integrity of the word of God. The issue is: Does God speak the truth?

In the temptation of Christ, the question is posed indirectly. The devil says to Jesus, "If you be the Son of God, command this stone that it be made bread" (Luke 4:3). He does not come and say to Jesus, "*Since* you are the Son of God, you can turn this stone into bread." He comes with a challenge: "*If* you be the Son of God . . ." Why would he take this approach? The answer is that the temptation came immediately after Jesus's baptism, at the end of which the heavens were opened and a voice from heaven was heard saying, "This is my beloved Son" (Matt. 3:17). Now the serpent comes, after Jesus's forty days of hunger, and suggests ever so subtly that perhaps Jesus is not the Son of God. "How could the heavenly Father let you be so lonely? How could the heavenly Father let you be so hungry?" That is the point of the temptation. "*If* you are the Son of God, prove it by turning these stones into bread."

What does Jesus say? "It is written, 'Man shall not live by bread alone, but by every word of God.' Why do you come to me and ask me to turn these stones into bread? I do not need to do that to know that I am the Son of God. God said that I am his Son. He does not lie. His word is truth. Do you not realize, Satan, that his word cannot be broken? His words are life. Right now the test of my life is the test of whom I believe. Do I believe you or do I believe my Father? How many times does my Father have to say I am his Son before I believe him? Can the fact that I am hungry change that reality?"

The issue with the first Adam was the truthfulness and the integrity of God's word, and Adam fell. The issue with the second Adam, Jesus, was the truthfulness and the fidelity of God's word, and Jesus stood.

Hallmark of Truth

There is a crisis of the principles of logic and reason within the Christian faith today and in the Christian community. People will accept contradictions. For instance, Emil Brunner says that contradiction is the hallmark of truth. According to Brunner, our theology has to live in the midst of a tension of dialectics where we affirm one thing with one hand and deny it with the other. Brunner claims that this is the nature of the mysterious complex of truth. Truth is so high, so wonderful, so marvelous that not only can it be mysterious from time to time, not only can it be paradoxical from time to time, not only may it be sprinkled here and there with irony and complexity, but the very hallmark of truth is contradiction. "There is no God, and Mary is his mother." That is sound theology, according to Brunner and many other people.

But is it? Not at all! Contradiction is the hallmark of the lie, not of the truth. Aristotle did not invent the law of contradiction; he merely defined it. And even within Aristotle's thinking, the law of contradiction was not set up as a metaphysical system that could stand upon itself. Logic is not a science in and of itself. It is only a tool that makes meaningful discourse possible. Without it there is no test of truth.

Let us suppose for a moment that God's word can violate the law of contradiction. Satan comes to Eve and says, "You shall not die." She says to herself, "Well, let's see. That other fellow who was here, who created me, said that if I eat of that tree I will die—whatever that means. But now this interesting creature has come to me, and he says that I will *not* die. I do not understand how I can die and not die in the same way and at the same time. This sounds like a contradiction. But contradiction is the hallmark of truth. And God is a God of truth. So this must be a messenger from God telling me to eat of the tree."

You see, when you throw away the law of contradiction, you not only throw away any possibility of determining the difference between truth and the lie, but you throw away any possibility of knowing the difference between sin and righteousness, because sin is a denial of righteousness. Sin is the opposite of obedience; it is disobedience. So if a statement can be both true and not true at the same time, then we can be both obedient and disobedient at the same time and God has no possible basis upon which to judge us or redeem us.

But Jesus was not going to fall for that. He said, "Wait a minute! Man shall not live by bread alone, but by every word of God, and I cannot obey the word of God and obey you at the same time."

The devil then took him to a high mountain and showed him all the kingdoms of the world. The devil said, "All this power will I give you, and the glory of them: for that is delivered unto me; and to whomsoever I will I give it. If you therefore will worship me, all shall be yours" (Luke 4:6–7).

Jesus answered him, "Get you behind me, Satan: for it is written, You shall worship the Lord your God, and him only shall you serve" (Luke 4:8).

And Satan said, "Yes, yes, I know. I've read the Book. I know it's written that you shall—you know—'serve the Lord your God.' But look, Jesus, how long ago was that written? What was the cultural context in which it was written? Why, you're even living under a misguided notion of who wrote it. Are you trying to tell me now, in our liberated society, that you are going to stand here and face the possibility of death from starvation over a technical point of obedience to an outmoded principle? Don't you know, Jesus, that there are no absolutes? Don't you know, Jesus, that Moses's statement is only the reflection of a naive herdsman in a Midianite culture centuries ago, and that it does not apply to our sophisticated culture today? Just bow down for a second.

"Jesus, if this were an article upon which your church would stand or fall, I can understand your reluctance. But we're not debating justification by faith; all we are talking about is a few loaves and a few stones—just a little thing. Look at your record. Forty days you went without eating! That's in the Guinness *Book of World Records*. You've done your job. How are you possibly going to relate to the people you're preaching to? You won't be one of them. You'll scare them. You'll threaten them. You've got to learn to bend. You're too narrow. All you do is sit there and recite to me, 'It is written, it is written, it is written.' What do you worship—the paper? You're not talking to a book right now; you're talking to a real person! Come on and worship me."

Then Satan says, "You're religious; I can see that. You're a Bible-believing fundamentalist; I can see that. Let's go to Jerusalem. I'm not going to drag you down into the ghettos of Philadelphia. We're going to Jerusalem, to the temple. We'll go to the center of religious concern where you'll be right at home, Jesus."

So Satan takes Jesus and sets him on the pinnacle of the temple. And he says, "If you are the Son of God, cast yourself down from here, because, Jesus, the Bible says that God will give his angels charge over you. In their hands they will bear you up lest you dash your foot against a stone. I'm not asking you to worship me now, to bow down to me. All I want you to do is put the Bible to the test. If you are the Son of God, then certainly the Bible gives you the freedom to put God to the test. Let's put out a fleece. Let's see if God really meant what he said. Let's verify his promise in the arena of space and time. Jump off the temple. Didn't God say that his angels would be with you? What do you think would happen, Jesus, if you did jump off the temple?"

"I believe that if I fell off the temple, heaven and earth would be mobilized to protect me," Jesus answers. "I believe my Father's word that he would give his angels charge over me. At my command I could have legions of angels coming here to minister to me. But God did not command me to go around giving ostentatious displays of my splendor and my glory. The commission he has given me is a commission of suffering, ignominy, humiliation and death. Your procedure does not fit into the commission that has been given to me. And if you will recall what the Scripture says, Satan, it says that I am not to put God to the test. It is one thing to put out a fleece in attempting to discover that which God has not revealed. But to test that which God has revealed is to insult the integrity of his word, and I will not do it.

"All you have done is to build your case, Satan, on the basis of one Scripture text taken in isolation, not tested by the rest of Scripture. But don't you see that the Book I obey is a Book that is coherent? One part cannot be set in contrast to another or in contradiction to another. Scripture is interpreted by Scripture."

Ironically, we read at the end of the verse that "when the devil had ended all the temptation, he departed from him for a season." That is all that Luke tells us. But when we go to the other Gospels we read that when Satan vanished the angels appeared and ministered to Christ and fed him. They vindicated him, but he had to wait for that vindication. He had to suffer before he was vindicated. He had to be insulted. Before he realized that vindication, he had to know what it means to go through the valley of the shadow of death and to be isolated in the wilderness. But he had made a decision that he would live by every word that comes from the mouth of God.

No Treason to Christ

That is what Reformation theology is all about: that our authority is nothing less and nothing more than the Word of

God. It cannot be compromised. It cannot be relativized. It cannot be culturized. But on the basis of that Word we live.

Many times I have had people say to me, "But if you live without compromising, you will destroy your career . . . you will destroy your vocation . . . you will lose your congregation . . . you will make enemies . . . you might even end up in the arena with the lions." But when people say that to me I hear again the voice of Satan. Sometimes people say to me, "You're too narrow, too rigid, too brittle! You're out of touch with contemporary culture! You're out of touch with the mainstream of human existence! Why don't you get in line and get with it?"

But what I go to bed at night sweating about in the presence of Christ is not my brittleness, narrowness, or rigidness. It is that when I see myself in the mirror of his Word I know that I have compromised that Word a hundred times that day. I am so easily intimidated, so easily threatened by all the forces in this world that would undo me. I know what Jesus was talking about when he said to his disciple, "Simon, Simon, behold, Satan has desired to have you, that he may sift you as wheat" (Luke 22:31), for I have been sifted and shaken. I have denied Christ not thrice but again and again and again. Then I see my champion, alone and hungry, not standing there with the armor of his divine nature warding off the darts of Satan, but in his humanity, saying, "It is written, it is written, it is written." That is my hero. That is the hero of the Reformation. It is there that we see the practical character of the Word of God, that we know the difference between the truth and a lie, and that we know that our lives are at stake on the basis of the truth of God.

Those who have committed themselves to the reconstruction and renewal of the Reformed faith in our day must be able to stand strong and unshakable in the contemporary wilderness and firmly say no to those who would cause us to commit treason against Christ.

8

The Key to Knowing God

RALPH L. KEIPER

IN THE *Institutes* Calvin suggests that we should be familiar with three great attributes of God the Father: his love, his judgment, and his justice. "Certainly these three things are especially necessary for us to know: mercy, on which alone the salvation of us all rests; judgment, which is daily exercised against wrongdoers, and in even greater severity awaits them to their everlasting ruin; justice, whereby believers are preserved, and are most tenderly nourished."[1]

In his commentaries, after stating a fact Calvin immediately leaves his own opinion and goes to the Word of God for authority. So now, as I follow in his footsteps, I turn to that Book. Let us look at these three attributes—the lovingkindness of God, the judgment of God, and the righteousness of God—the attributes that Calvin assures us we should know.

1. John Calvin, *Institutes of the Christian Religion*, ed. John T. McNeill and trans. Ford Lewis Battles (Philadelphia: The Westminster Press, 1960), 98.

God So Loved

How can I better begin a discussion of the lovingkindness of God than by turning to that great verse from John's Gospel: "For God so loved the world, that he gave his only begotten Son, that whosoever believes in him should not perish, but have everlasting life" (3:16)? Words intrigue me, and one of the words that intrigues me in this verse is the word *so*. God *so* loved the world. Since I was fascinated by this word, I began to search the commentaries. I even to a degree began to search Calvin's writings. To my horror I discovered that at this point Calvin never commented on what I really wanted to know! So I was forced back to the Bible. One day I found what I was looking for. In John 17:23 our divine Lord says, "[I pray] that the world may know that you have sent me, and have loved them, as you have loved me."

I have no doubt that, if asked, parents would admit the love they show their individual children is not impartial. It may be *almost* impartial, but not quite. This impartiality may be caused by the brilliance of a son in comparison to the other children, or the beauty of a daughter, or some other outstanding characteristic. For some reason one of the children is more favored than the others. But God knows no favorite, even where his Son is concerned. He loves us with the same love with which he loves his Son.

He saw me ruined in the fall,
Yet loved me notwithstanding all,
And saved me from my lost estate,
His lovingkindness is so great![2]

Yes, his lovingkindness is manifested in the gift. God so loved the world that he gave his *only begotten Son*. And how did

2. Samuel Medley, "Awake, My Soul, to Joyful Lays," 1782.

he give him? Did he give him that he might come to condemn us? Did he give him that he might show his anger? Did he give him that he might put us on notice that we shall be eternally lost? Look at John 3:17: "For God sent not his Son into the world to condemn the world; but that the world through him might be saved." God's desire is not to show his wrath but to show his love, mercy, and grace.

This gives us great security. It is a wonderful thing, when we stop to think about it, that God in his marvelous grace sent his Son to show his love. "Herein is love, not that we loved God, but that he loved us, and sent his Son to be the propitiation for our sins" (1 John 4:10). God's love differs from ours in that it has no ulterior motives. He did not choose us or elect us to see how much he could get out of us, because he foreknew that we were a total loss. But he elected us, chose us, and saved us that he might give to us what we need, making us new creatures in Christ Jesus. The miracle is that God loved us. In contrast, my love for God is often a selfish love. I see this in my prayers. So many times my prayer is, "Give me this, give me that; bless me here, bless me there."

In the forty years that I have been born again, I think I have heard only one truly honest prayer from the pulpit. It was in a Baptist church in Newark, New Jersey. The old minister was praying for a member of his congregation who was sick unto death. He prayed, in his old Scots' brogue, "Dear Lord Jesus, we ask that in thy sovereign grace thou wilt raise up our sister who has been a blessing among us. Recover her to health and strength that we might know her fellowship and continue to be blessed with her testimony. But, oh, our heavenly Father, if it be thy sovereign will to take her to thyself, line our earthly sorrow with thy heavenly joy, that we might be the blessing to others in the hour of our grief that she has been to us when she was among us."

It is not difficult to believe in the sovereignty of God when things are going our way, but this dear man believed in the sovereignty of God when things were going God's way!

First John 4:10 is theology; 1 John 4:11 is practice. "Beloved, if God so loved us, we ought also to love one another." Love one another without an angle? Love one another when it may be to our disadvantage? Love one another for your sake, Lord? That is it exactly. That is the practicality of God's love, obedience to love no matter what.

Answerable to God

Let us look now at the judgment of God. Calvin said to us, you will remember, that God's judgment is that which he daily exercises upon the wicked and which in the future he will manifest in their eternal separation from him. Does that mean that God delights in judgment? I do not think so.

Look at Romans 3:19. God, in his marvelous grace, has done everything in his power to keep men from going to hell. The very fact that he has sent the Lord Jesus Christ to die for mankind is proof of that. But then he has done something else. He has given the law, and the purpose of the law is to judge. And I think that the law has been given not so much to condemn us to be eternally separated from him as to judge us that we might (in love) be forced back to him. "Now we know that what things soever the law says, it says to them who are under the law: that every mouth may be stopped, and all the world may become guilty [the Greek says, I believe, 'answerable'] before God. Therefore, by the deeds of the law there shall no flesh be justified in his sight: for by the law is the knowledge of sin." What does this mean? It means that by the law our sin is imputed to us so that we must face him with it, for not only are we sinners by nature, but we are sinners by law as well.

Let me illustrate. Under most circumstances Mrs. Keiper is normal. But she has her moments. When we lived in Philadelphia, she would drive me to my office at *Eternity* magazine, and then she would drive to her office a block away. We would drive through Fairmount Park and cross Girard Avenue. At a small street there was a sign: S-T-O-P. She drove as though it read S-L-O-W. I said to her on one occasion, "Darling, even I can see that that sign says S-T-O-P. Why do you drive as though it says S-L-O-W?"

"Who's driving the car?" she retorted.

Now, I am not an Anglican or even an Episcopalian, but I developed a liturgy. I began to sing to myself, "There's sin in you, there's sin in you, there's sin in you." One morning we came down through the park, crossed Girard Avenue, and reached the intersection where the sign still read S-T-O-P. Mrs. Keiper drove as though it read S-L-O-W. As we coasted into the intersection, we heard a whistle and, knowing my theology, I was forced to change my liturgy from "There's sin in you" to "There's sin on you," because, you see, she was now a sinner by law also. And fifteen dollars went to the traffic court instead of to Wanamaker's!

God's laws are absolute. They are never relative, as man's laws are apt to be. *Every* man and *every* woman who has come into conflict with God's law is answerable to him. But God, even as our judge, does not desire us to be lost.

Let us go back to Genesis 3. There we read that Satan, that subtle serpent, caused Eve to doubt the love, fairness, and justice of God. From that day to this, men have been victims of Satan's malicious, devilish half-truth. When they do wrong, the only thing they sense is a God of wrath; they cannot understand a God of love.

Some time ago I was in a friend's home. The children were playing upstairs. In the process they got into their grandfather's room and knocked over some very lovely carved vases he had brought from his native Sweden. In a moment those beautiful vases had become smashed vases. The children came downstairs crying. When their mother asked why they were crying, the reply was, "We've smashed Grandpa's vases. They're broken."

The mother reassured them, "Don't cry. Grandpa won't whip you."

And do you know what the children said? "That's the trouble; we know he won't!"

Somehow the human heart cannot stand the grace of God. Oh, if God would just show his wrath, we could fight him back! We could go to hell fighting! But what can you do with his grace? What can you do with his love? How can you retaliate?

Preserved and Cherished

Calvin says that we must not only know the loving-kindness and the judgment of God, but we must also know the righteousness of God, that righteousness by which the faithful are preserved and cherished. How preserved are we? How cherished?

Not so long ago I was riding in a plane. I could tell by his accent that my seat companion was Jewish. As I became acquainted with him, I discovered him to be a realtor from our hometown of Denver. And by his conversation I judged that he was a wonderful man, full of good works. Now in the old days I would have argued with him. I would have said, "You can't be saved by works." And he might have said, "Where are you from, Mars?" But instead I said,

"Mr. W——, I take it that you are a wonderful man. I know that you are telling me the truth, because I have heard of you over our television and radio and have read about you in our newspapers. You sound as though you're as good as I am! We ought to be very, very good friends!"

So he said, "Why not?"

Then I said to him, "Mr. W——, do you know that God loves good men? In fact, do you realize that the Torah indicates this?"

"The Torah? You know the Torah, the first five books?"

"Yes," I said. "I read the Old Testament and am conversant with it. I know that God loves good men."

He asked, "How good must you be?"

"As good as God, for the text says, 'Be ye holy; for I am holy.'"[3]

"I'm not that good," he replied.

"Well, what are you going to do?"

"Since you make the problem," he said, "you make the suggestion."

"Well," I said, "in the Old Testament Israel had sacrifices. And if their heart was right, they could bring a sacrifice and, taking God at his word, know that he would accept it. Abraham believed God and it was counted to him for righteousness."

"Well," he said, "we don't have any of those sacrifices."

"You're in trouble."

"Don't tell me what I know; give me a solution."

"Well," I said, "I am a Gentile Baptist, but I know a Jewish Baptist who has some advice."

"You do?"

"Yes, I do. One day as he was standing on the bank of a river a figure came by and he interrupted himself to say, 'Behold the Lamb of God, which takes away the sin of the world.'[4]

3. 1 Peter 1:16.
4. John 1:29.

Furthermore, another great Hebrew on one occasion said, 'Even Christ our passover is sacrificed for us.'[5]"

Did my new friend get angry? Did he turn away? No! He said, "Tell me more."

So we went back to the Torah. We explored that—I thought he probably would not know the New Testament, and I thought, too, in a slightly mercenary way, that if I told him of the Torah on the plane he would invite me to his house for dinner, and then we could talk about the New Testament.

Notice Romans 3:24: "Being justified freely by his grace through the redemption that is in Christ Jesus." Here we have two tremendous theological terms: "being *justified* freely by his *grace*." It is one thing to be graciously forgiven; it is quite another to be justly forgiven. For the sake of illustration, suppose I am a pastor in Jersey City and a friend of the mayor. The mayor says to me, "Keiper, I'm looking for votes. There are probably votes in your parish. If I get those votes, I may be able to do you a few favors. If you drive where you should not, or park where you ought not, and get a ticket from the police, take it down to the traffic court and I will take care of it." Now let us assume that I get forty traffic tickets while this particular mayor is in office. I take them down to City Hall and there I am graciously forgiven. Then the election comes along, and suddenly there is a new mayor who hates the former mayor. Let us assume that I now receive a phone call.

"Reverend?" a voice inquires.

"Yes."

"Have you ever parked your car where it should not have been parked?"

"Yes."

"What did you do about it?"

5. 1 Corinthians 5:7.

"Oh, I got a number of tickets and took them down to City Hall, and the mayor graciously forgave me."

"Great! But there's a new administration in office now, including a new mayor. Please come down and pay up. Your name is still on the blotter, and there is no receipt marked 'Paid.'"

You see, although I may have been *graciously* forgiven I was not *justly* forgiven, and from the law's point of view I would still have to pay for every one of those violations.

It is the same spiritually. If we were only to be graciously forgiven, Christ would not have had to die. But God had said, justly, "The soul that sins, it shall die" (Ezek. 18:20). God declared, "The wages of sin is death" (Rom. 6:23). God could not graciously forgive us because it would have violated his holiness and his righteousness. And if I may use a human term, *God had a problem on his hands!* How was he to exercise his love, his mercy, and his grace without violating his holiness and his righteousness? God called a meeting. He called the Father, the Son, and the Holy Spirit. What a meeting it was! The outcome was absolutely fantastic! The Father said, "I want to exercise my mercy. I want to exercise my love. I want to manifest my grace. But how can I do so in the light of my integrity, my holiness, my justice?"

The Son said, "I understand. You said, 'The soul that sins, it shall die.' You said, 'The wages of sin is death.' I will go, I will die, so that you can show your love and your mercy without violating your righteousness and your holiness."

So we turn to Hebrews 10:5–7 and read that as he was coming into the world the Lord said, "Sacrifice and offering you [did not desire], but a body have you prepared me: in burnt offerings and sacrifices for sin you have had no pleasure. . . . Lo, I come (in the volume of the book it is written of me) to do your will, O God." And what was that will? It was what our divine Lord himself says in Matthew 20:28: "The Son of man came not to be ministered unto, but to minister, and to give his life a ransom for many."

If anyone should ever look at the record to see what is there in our behalf, he will discover that as far as the east is from the west, so far has God removed our transgressions from us. Our sins have been completely obliterated.

Coming from a poor family, I recall how my mother always had to borrow money. Household finance, we called it. We paid more interest than principal. Well, as a boy, I took a book to the bank and each month I entered in it what we paid, including the interest. I did this for eighteen months, and I promised God that if I could avoid it I would never go into debt, because it is a miserable experience. We never had any money to call our own; it always belonged to somebody else. Well, when I made the last payment, it was terrific! First, they entered in the amount I paid, then they stamped on my book, "Paid in full," and gave it back to me. Then they handed to me through the window their book against me. And *that* said, "Paid in full." They no longer had a record against us.

What should these three attributes of God do for us, his loving-kindness, his judgment, his justice? They should cause our hearts to sing:

> Arise, my soul, arise,
> Shake off thy guilty fears;
> The bleeding Sacrifice
> In my behalf appears:
> Before the throne my surety stands,
> My name is written on his hands.[6]

6. Charles Wesley, "Arise, My Soul, Arise," 1742.

9

Discerning the Will of God

R.C. SPROUL

WHENEVER WE talk about knowing or discerning the will of God, we are immediately faced with the problem of ambiguity in the meaning of the word *will.* I know that if there is anything tedious and repugnant to the layman, it is the theologian's habit of making fine distinctions. But I appeal to the theologian's prerogative to make a few distinctions, because it is by making distinctions that knowledge is possible and our understanding of things is sharpened.

The Wills of God

When we come to the biblical text and look at the word *will,* we find that there are several meanings attached to the term in the Bible. This has led theologians throughout the history of the church to give us such distinctions as that between the *decretive* and the *preceptive* wills of God or between the *revealed* and the *secret* wills of God. The distinction that I would like to hone in on briefly is between what we call the *sovereign* or *efficacious* will of God and the *disposition* of God.

When we talk about the sovereign or efficacious will of God, it sounds like theological jargon. But what we mean by the sovereign or efficacious will of God is that determination by which God sovereignly wills something to come to pass that, therefore, indeed does come to pass through the sheer efficacy, force, or power of that will. We often say, "That's the will of God." What we mean is that God himself has brought this to pass. It is not an accident. It is not fortuitous. It is not a cosmic contingency. Rather, God has acted. Was it an accident that Jesus Christ went to the cross? Or did God send his Son into the world to die? The answer is that God willed it. By his efficacious will he brought to pass what he desired to bring to pass.

But the Bible also speaks of the will of God in terms of his disposition. This is that which is pleasing to God. It is what God favors or what delights him, but it does not always come to pass.

To illustrate the question at hand, let us take a passage in the New Testament that every good Calvinist knows is in the Bible. The reason he knows it is in the Bible is that every Arminian constantly reminds him of it: "The Lord is . . . not willing that any should perish" (2 Peter 3:9). In what sense is God not willing that any should perish? In the sovereign, efficacious sense by which he brings to pass that which he will bring to pass? If we assign that meaning to the text, if we say that God is not willing in that sense that any should perish, then the clear implication of the passage is that none will perish. If God is not willing in the sovereign, final, decretive, or ultimate sense that any should perish, then, obviously, none will perish.

But do we have any problems with assigning that particular meaning to that text? Yes, because the rest of the New

Testament seems to indicate that in the final analysis there will be those who perish.

Well, then, is there any other way in which the Bible speaks of the will of God that might make sense to us in this text? What about the sense of will as God's disposition? Does that fit? I think it does, for in this case the verse means that God is not pleased with the death of the wicked. God does not get satisfaction from the death of those who are impenitent. God does not enjoy sentencing the lost. A feeble human analogy would be a judge who is called on by virtue of his office to execute a sentence but does so reluctantly and in a spirit of grief.

So whenever we say, "How do I know the will of God?" or "What is the will of God for my life?" we must know what we are seeking. Are we trying to find out what is pleasing to him? Or are we trying to find out his secret counsel?

God's Preceptive Will

If we are speaking of God's preceptive will, much can be said, for God has revealed to us what he desires for our behavior. God wills our righteousness. God wills our obedience. And the law of God clearly reflects something of his will in the preceptive sense, the sense of his disposition. Here we may turn to Psalm 1. In it God pronounces his blessing upon the person who "walks not in the counsel of the ungodly, nor stands in the way of sinners, nor sits in the seat of the scornful" (v. 1), those who are the mockers and cynics of this world. God is not pleased with that type of behavior. It is not his will that you mock him. But God puts his benediction upon the one whose "delight is in the law of the LORD" and who meditates on it "day and night" (v. 2).

Do you think David meditated on the law of God day and night? I know he did. He had to. For he was a man who was responsible not only to be a military leader to the people of Israel, to protect their borders, but also to execute judgment and righteousness as the king of the people of God. David was called upon to make decision after decision in the name of God. A man with that kind of awesome responsibility is driven to meditating on the law of God day and night. So if you want to know the will of God for your life, if you want to know what is pleasing to God, what he delights in, enjoys, and approves, then you must meditate on his Word day and night.

In the Old Testament, if somebody wanted to discover the particular will of God for his life, there were many different ways God could reveal it. God revealed himself to Moses in a burning bush. What a story! Moses was out there in the wilderness, walking along, minding his own business. He had long forgotten the problems and trials he knew back in Egypt when suddenly he walked past this bush. It was burning! That was not too significant. He looked a little bit later, and it was still burning; but the bush was not consumed. Soon the bush started talking: "Moses, Moses. . . . Put off your shoes from off your feet, for the place whereon you stand is holy ground" (Ex. 3:4, 5). No man ever got out of his shoes as fast as Moses did in the wilderness that day!

And then you know what happened. The bush revealed itself to him. It was the Lord God omnipotent speaking. And God said in that theophany, "Moses, I want you to go down to the courts of Egypt, to the imperial leader of the most important and influential nation on the face of this earth today, and I want you to tell him to freely and gratuitously release the most lucrative work force that any nation has ever employed—the free labor of the Israelites. I want you to go down to him and say, 'Let my people go!'"

Moses said, "I'm not sure that I want to take that on."

God said, "You go. Don't tell me that you don't know how to speak. I'll take care of that. You go."

So Moses went, knocked at the door of the palace of Pharaoh, and there found a secretary of appointments. He asked Moses, "What's your name?"

"Moses."

"What do you want?"

"I want to see the Pharaoh."

"Do you have an appointment?"

"No."

"Who sent you?"

"Well, I was talking to this bush!"

Now, if you think you have problems trying to explain to people how you feel that God has led you to a particular decision, remember Moses. I do not know how he ever got in to see Pharaoh, but he did. And then imagine him telling Pharaoh the same story! No wonder it took the plagues of Egypt to convince Pharaoh that Moses was serious.

So we have God leading his people by means of a theophany. Moreover, he leads them through the wilderness by a pillar of cloud and fire. He speaks to people in dreams in the Old Testament and in the New Testament. For example, he sends Mary and Joseph fleeing from the wrath of Herod by warning them in a dream. We see the fleece of Gideon. We see the strange use of the Urim and the Thummim and the casting of lots in Scripture. But even then, despite these extraordinary manifestations of the guidance and leading of God, the king of Israel still meditates on the Word day and night. So we conclude that even in Old Testament situations the primary method of learning and understanding the will of God was through searching the Scripture diligently.

I am not going to say that God does not lead us in these days by extraordinary means. I am sure that he does. But it is rare. Even in the lives of the greatest saints of history, extraordinary leading is not normal. The normal means by which God leads his people is through the clarity of his written Word.

Specific Problems

Many students come to me in tremendous anxiety, asking: "Whom should I marry?" or "What should my career be?" or "Where should I live?" These are obviously profound concerns, and I try to help them with these questions because, if we want to be pleasing to God, we certainly want to do with our lives what God will approve. But how do we know what he wants in these areas? We have not seen any burning bushes. The pillar of cloud is no longer around. We wonder about dreams. Gideon's fleece has long since vanished. How do we know?

Well, Scripture reveals the will of God for our life in several ways. First of all, it limits our options. Is it the will of God that I become a bookie? Is it the will of God that a woman become a prostitute? The answers to these questions are obvious, because the Scripture limits us at this point.

Then again, the Bible gives us principles. This is necessary too, because at many points the Scripture has not limited the options available to us. The principles are there to guide us. Not long ago I talked to Bishop Alfred Stanway, who has spent most of his life in Africa. He told me of meeting another missionary in Africa on one occasion. The man had not shaved. Bishop Stanway said to him, "Do you know that you didn't shave this morning?"

The man said happily, "Yes, I know I didn't shave. The reason I didn't shave is that I didn't feel like shaving today, and I haven't made a decision yet whether I'm going to shave or not. I want my life to be spontaneous. I want my life to be free from regimentation. So I don't decide about shaving until the Holy Spirit moves me to decide about shaving."

Bishop Stanway said to the man, "Let me make a suggestion. Let me suggest to you that starting tomorrow morning you agree with yourself that from this day forth you are going to shave as soon as you get out of bed every day for the rest of your life."

The man asked, "Why should I do that? There's no fun in that."

Stanway replied, "I just can't stand the thought of having you go through the agony of making decisions like that every single day of your life. If you make a decision to live by principle, you have saved yourself three hundred and sixty-five decisions a year about shaving, and you can give your decision-making agonies to more significant questions."

I say this because so often, it seems, we are more concerned about discovering the will of God about where we should live, whom we should marry, what job we should take, and so on, than about mastering the principles of life that God wills for each one of us.

The man who lives by the principles of God, who searches the Scripture, who meditates on the law day and night, as David said, is like a tree planted by living waters. Think of that image! Have you ever seen an arid wilderness, a barren landscape, where one scraggly withered tree with two or three leaves is stretching and fighting to stay alive? The tree is not stable. Unless it gets water and nutrients, it is soon going to decay and perish. That is one kind of tree.

Or have you ever seen a massive tree springing from gigantic roots, firmly planted on the banks of a moving stream where the nutrients are there every day increasing the strength and force of the tree? You see that tree stretch itself up toward heaven and send out branch upon branch, limb upon limb. The fruit it bears is abundant. That is what David says the man who meditates on the law is like. He is like a tree that produces fruit in its season. The ungodly are not like that. They are like chaff which the wind drives away, unstable, tossed to and fro with every opinion and with everybody's advice. They do not have any idea how to discern the will of God, and they become preoccupied with questions like which city they should live in rather than how to be an obedient Christian wherever they might happen to live.

The most difficult decisions are always between rival goods. It is one thing when we have to make a decision between that which is evil and that which is good. The answer to that is clear from Scripture. It is the will of God that we do that which is righteous. But what if our options are both righteous, are both approved by God? That is a more difficult decision to make, but—and this is my point—it is less threatening. Because in the final analysis, we are not responsible to know what the secret will of God is. We are free to choose either course, as long as they are both pleasing to God.

Since we are talking about the secret counsel again, may I be so blunt as to say it in a simple way: the secret counsel of God is none of our business! I do not know any way to know the secret counsel of God in terms of our personal histories until after the fact.

Vocations

When we come to the question of the stewardship of our lives, we need practical suggestions. Thus, in Romans we find Paul calling us to make a sober analysis of our gifts and talents, that we might not think too highly of ourselves, nor too lowly. False humility does nothing in terms of leading us in the stewardship of our lives before God. Again, we must go to the Scriptures, for the Scriptures give us principles by which we can make this evaluation. Finally, we must go to the body of Christ and ask our friends to be honest with us. We can ask, "Do you see any gifts in my life?" The Bible says that, if I see the gift of teaching in you, I should encourage you to teach and should not stand in your way.

Moreover, if I have the gift of evangelism and you have the gift of teaching, I am not to go to you and say, "Why are you not more involved in evangelism?" That is what goes on in the evangelical world because we esteem our own gifts so highly. We are always encouraging everybody else to do what we are doing. We think that what we are doing is the only thing that really counts in the kingdom of God. But we need to apply the principle of self-analysis not only to ourselves but to each other. If I see you with a gift, I should encourage you to develop that gift. And you should encourage me to develop my gift.

One of the greatest tragedies in the church today is that we leave the call to the pastoral ministry to a direct or supernatural experience while the New Testament principle of the call of the pastor is the call through men. I know of no apostles directly and immediately called by God since the first century. But the apostles themselves were instructed to call out men from the congregation, asking them to take a serious look at the possibility of ministry. We should encourage people who are gifted leaders to come to the place of leadership in the church of Jesus Christ. We are not stepping on the providence of God if we do that.

However, if you go to a person and say, "I know that this is the will of God for *your* life," you had better be careful. I was unemployed at one time and was looking for what I should be doing. I was in agony and prayer every night. During that time I had five different people come to me about five different job possibilities that I was considering, and these people said with all earnestness, "R.C., the Spirit has revealed to me that you are to take such and such a job." But they were all different jobs. I got to thinking about that. Does God really want me to hold a job in five different cities, all of which are full-time jobs? I liked the idea of gaining all five salaries. That was not so bad. But somehow I came to the conclusion that at least four of those five people did not know the mind of Christ for me. Yet they presumed to enter into my life as I was wrestling and struggling, as best as I knew how, and dared to say that they *knew* God wanted me to do something.

This works another way when we claim that God leads us to do certain things. One of the reasons why we talk like this is that it is part of our evangelical vocabulary. But another reason is that we often want to stop criticism or evaluation. Sober analysis usually ceases whenever we decide we want to do something and therefore tell everybody that the Spirit is leading us to do it. We set up a spiritual wall, saying, "If you question my judgment, what you are doing is attacking me at the very heart of my spirituality." Do not do that! I believe that in many cases we come perilously close to blaspheming the Holy Spirit by some of the things we have attributed to him in claiming his leadership or guidance.

I do not know how many women and men involved in an extramarital affair have come to me and told me that they prayed about it and God gave them peace. They claimed that the Spirit of God actually led them to violate their own marriages. That is very close to blasphemy. It is at least a serious slander of God the Holy Spirit.

Having Done All

So I plead with you to be careful about the casual, easy way in which you claim the leading of God before the Christian community. To discern the will of God in your life is a very, very serious matter. It must be done soberly, not through magic, superstition, or hunches. But notice that if after you have done your homework—after you have read the Word, consulted the elders of your Christian community, asked the whole body of

Christ—everyone agrees that you can serve him just as well as a physician or as a lawyer, then go either way. And go in peace, knowing that you have the blessing of God. Having done all, you stand. You do not live the rest of your life in anxiety over whether you should have been a physician or should have been this or that. God does not expect us to be able to penetrate into his secret counsels. He does expect us to be diligent, responsible stewards of his Word and of the principles he sets down for discerning what is pleasing to him.

I would like to close by saying that I once read an article written by the late Dr. Benjamin B. Warfield on the leading of the Holy Spirit. I was jolted by that particular essay because I had always approached the question of the Spirit in a different way. Dr. Warfield painstakingly and meticulously, in his inimitable style as a careful New Testament scholar, waded through all the New Testament texts that deal with the leading of the Holy Spirit and came up with a very strong conclusion. It was that the primary meaning of the leading of the Spirit in the New Testament is the leading of Christian people, not to San Francisco, not to marrying Betty rather than Julie or Frank rather than Tom, but into sanctification. "This is the will of God, even your sanctification" (1 Thess. 4:3), and that can happen in San Francisco, Chicago, or Philadelphia. It can happen if you are married to Ruth, Mary, or Shirley. It may be God's hidden counsel that you marry Shirley. But if this is his hidden, ultimate, efficacious, and sovereign will, you can be sure that this efficacious and sovereign decree will be enacted and that you will marry the right person. Do not worry about it.

Let us get on with seeking the kingdom of God, which is the main and central business of our lives and the main and central business of God the Holy Spirit.

10

Disobedience and God's Sovereignty

JAMES MONTGOMERY BOICE

ALTHOUGH GOD has permitted men to disobey him, he nevertheless has established that their disobedience must be according to his laws. This applies to those who are unregenerate, but it also applies to those who are God's people. We disobey. But when we disobey, it is according to the laws which God has laid down to govern disobedience.

However, we do not always understand how these laws operate. For example, God tells us that we are to do a certain thing and we say, "I don't want to do it." What happens at that point? Does God say, "Well, you are my child; I love you, and so if you do not want to obey me, I certainly do not want to insist on anything unpleasant; we will just forget about the commandment"? It does not seem that this is the way he operates. However, God does not seem to say either, "You *are* going to do it! Therefore I will smash you down so you have to." God does not seem to take either of these two approaches. So how does God operate when we as Christians determine that we do not want to do what he wants us to do? In order to look at this subject, I want to deal with a biblical story that was written about this problem. It is the story of Jonah.

A Great Commission

The basis for the story is the commission of God to Jonah. We recognize Jonah's story to be our story because the commission he was given is precisely the commission we are given when we are told to go into all the world and teach the gospel of Christ to every creature.

Jonah 1:2 says, "Arise, go to Nineveh, that great city, and cry against it; for their wickedness is come up before me." There are three verbs in this commission: first, "arise"—that is, we do not belong sitting in the pew indefinitely, listening to good sermons, exciting though they may be; second, "go"—there is a world out there that we must go to; and third, "cry"—that is, we must verbalize our witness. It is not enough just to live our testimony. That is what Paul Little has called *pre-evangelism*. It is essential, but it is not enough. Rather, we must speak the things that the Lord Jesus Christ has already spoken to us. This is what Jonah was told to do. But we read in the third verse that the problem began when Jonah said in his heart, "I will not do it."

Perhaps the most significant word in the entire book of Jonah is the word that begins verse 3 in our English Bibles, the word *but*. Verse 3 reads, "But Jonah . . ." Then if we skip down another verse, we have *but* again; this time, however, it says, "But the LORD . . ." There is an enormous amount of theology here. Furthermore, if we go to the third chapter, we find a parallel at the point of Jonah's later obedience. In Jonah 3:3 we read, "So Jonah . . ." Then in verse 5, "So the people of Nineveh believed

God." In other words, when Jonah said, "But," God had his "but" too. When Jonah said, "Yes," God also had his "yes" and brought blessing. The flow of the book is along these lines.

A Downhill Path

Jonah 1:3 brings us to the first of those principles that concern the operation of God's sovereignty in the disobedience of his children. It is the one that I alluded to briefly above. God has ordered things in such a way that when we disobey him we disobey according to his laws. This is evident in Romans 1, for example. Romans indicates that when men and women will not acknowledge God as the true God and worship him and be thankful to him as the Creator, they are inevitably launched on a path that leads them away from him and causes them to suffer the consequences, including the debasement of their own beings. Precisely the same thing occurs in Jonah 1.

In Jonah this principle is indicated in a poetic way by a repetition of the word *down*. Verse 3 says, "But Jonah rose up to flee unto Tarshish from the presence of the LORD, and went *down* to Joppa." The same verse adds that when he had found the ship he went *down* into it. Then, in verse 5, he went *down* into the sides of the ship; that is, he went into the lower recesses of the vessel. Finally, in Jonah 2:6, which describes what happened to him after he had been thrown overboard, Jonah says, "I went *down* to the bottoms of the mountains; the earth with her bars was about me for ever." Down, down, down, down! That is a lot of going down, but it is the inevitable course for anyone who runs away from God.

Notice that this is not what Jonah expected. If we had come to Jonah when he first disobeyed and had said to him, "Jonah, why are you setting out on this course that is going to take you downward?" Jonah would have answered, "I'm not going down; I'm going up! I'm going to improve my lot." But God says, "I have ordered my laws in such a way that regardless of what you think of the matter your course is going to be downhill." We can explain the unhappiness of many Christian people—their discouragements, lack of faith, and hardships—by the fact that at some point in their life they said, "I'm going to go my way rather than the way God has set before me."

Paying Your Bills

There is a second law of God's sovereignty here. The story says that when Jonah went down to Joppa he found a ship going to Tarshish and "paid the fare" (Jonah 1:3). Jonah found a ship going as far in the opposite direction from Nineveh as he could go. Tarshish was probably at the far end of the Mediterranean Sea. He said, "I am going to run away from the presence of the Lord." But he never got to Tarshish. Halfway there, the mariners threw him overboard, and he never got a refund on his ticket.

This causes me to reiterate a principle once stated by the late Donald Grey Barnhouse: When you run away from God, you never get to where you are going and you always pay your own bills. But when you go in God's way, you always get to where you are going and he pays the bills.

Jonah is an illustration of the first part of that principle. But there is also an excellent illustration of the second part in Scripture. It is the story of Moses, when he was just a baby, and Jochebed, who was Moses's mother. Moses's mother had received Moses as a special gift from God. She recognized that the time of the deliverance of her people had come. Perhaps she even imagined that Moses might be the deliverer. So she tried to save him from the soldiers who by order of the Pharaoh were determined to kill all the babies. According to the story, she hid the child for three months. But at the end of those months his cries were getting louder and she recognized that, if she kept him in her home, soon the soldiers would come by and hear the baby and would come in and take him out and kill him, as they had done with all the others. The thing that Jochebed most wanted in all the world was to have her child, to keep him and raise him. Yet she recognized that if God's will with her child was to be done, it would have to be by her giving him up to God to preserve in his own way. So, reluctantly perhaps, but in obedience to the will of God, she took the child and placed him in an ark down by the reeds in the river, stationing Moses's sister, Miriam, up on the hillside to see what would happen.

Pharaoh's daughter came down to the water and saw the ark. After it had been brought to shore by her servants, she opened it up, and there was the baby. The baby was crying. The tears touched the heart of Pharaoh's daughter, and she said, "This is one of the Hebrew babies, but we must not kill him. We will preserve this child. I will keep him. I will raise him as my son." Finally she said, "We will have to find a nurse for this baby."

About this time Miriam came down the hill. Miriam must have said something like this: "What do you have there in the basket?"

Pharaoh's daughter said, "It's a baby."

"A baby! Isn't that nice! Can I be of any help?"

Pharaoh's daughter said, "Yes, you can. We're going to need a nurse for the baby. Do you think you could find one?"

Miriam said, "I think maybe I could find someone to be his nurse."

Pharaoh's daughter replied, "Well, see what you can do." So Miriam started off and quite naturally got her mother and brought her back.

Now occurs the scene to which the story has been leading. Pharaoh's daughter is holding Moses in her arms, and Moses's mother arrives. Pharaoh's daughter is about to give the baby back to his mother without knowing it. In other words, Moses's mother is about to receive the thing she most wanted. Pharaoh's daughter hands the baby to Moses's mother and says, "I want you to take this child, raise him in your home as your own child and"—here is the phrase for which I tell the story—"I will give you your wages."

Moses's mother got what she most wanted, and God paid her bills. But Jonah, who had determined to run away from God, paid his own bills and never did get to where he was going. I repeat: If you run away from God, you never get to where you are going and you always pay your own bills. But if you go God's way, he guarantees that you get to where you are going and, furthermore, he pays the bills.

All that is in Jonah 1:3 and is in answer to this question of God's sovereignty in the matter of our disobedience. Here are basic spiritual laws. It is like jumping out of the window. If you do that, God does not have to intervene in any special way. You are just going to fall. Similarly, if you disobey God, the path will be downhill; you will not get where you want to go, and you will always have to pay your own expenses. All that is natural. That will happen without any special intervention of God at all.

Divine Intervention

Jonah 1:4 introduces God into the story in a supernatural way. God has been in the story all along—through the call to Jonah, through the establishment of his laws—but here, after Jonah has gotten on board ship, God intervenes in a supernatural way. He does this for two reasons: first of all, to go after Jonah and, second, to bring about his original purpose. So a second principle in the matter of disobedience and God's sovereignty is that God will accomplish his purposes anyway, even if we disobey. He can do it through judgment upon us in our disobedience. He can do it through blessing upon us in our obedience. But he will do it regardless.

The whole story of Jonah indicates this principle. God worked on Jonah, brought him to a position of repentance, recommissioned him, sent him to Nineveh, and brought about one of the greatest revivals in history. The whole city believed, from top to bottom, from the greatest to the least significant person. All this happened, interestingly enough, as part of God's sovereign plan. God indicated what he was going to do from the beginning. In the revival of Nineveh, Jonah was part of the blessing. But in an earlier episode, which we are going to consider next, Jonah missed the blessing.

The episode has to do with the mariners on the ship to Tarshish. They were pagans too, just like the people of Nineveh to whom Jonah did not want to preach. He did not want to preach to pagans because he did not want to carry a blessing to them. However, he was quite willing to take their service when they were carrying him away from God. This is true of all too many Christians. They do not want to preach to the world; they do not want to testify to those who need the gospel. But they are quite happy to use the world's services as they run away. Well, the mariners were serving Jonah, and Jonah was sleeping while they were heading into the storm. The fact that they were pagans is indicated in verse 5: "Then the mariners were afraid, and cried every man *unto his god*." That is, they worshiped the pagan gods of antiquity, and each man cried out to the god he thought could help him.

All this time Jonah was down in the ship asleep. But, finally, the chief pilot came to him and said, "I don't know who you are, and I don't know who your God is; but if we're going to get out of this, we're going to have to stick together. I want you to come up on board, and I want you to pray too." So, like those of the world who call upon God when in trouble, this pilot got Jonah to join in an all-night prayer meeting.

While the pilot was gone, the mariners gathered around and began to reason like this: "This is not a normal storm. We've been sailing the Mediterranean for many years, and we've never seen a storm like this. One of us has done something wrong, and God is after him. We need to find out who he is. Let's draw straws to find out who the guilty one is." They included Jonah in this lottery too. Then they drew straws, and the lot fell on Jonah.

Now it was no accident that it fell on Jonah. There is a verse in Proverbs that says that although men roll the dice, God makes the spots come up. "The lot is cast into the lap; but the whole disposing thereof is of the LORD" (Prov. 16:33). This is what happened to Jonah when the lot fell on him. So he was singled out, and immediately the mariners' questions came pouring out like a torrent: "Tell us, we pray you, for whose cause this evil is upon us; What is your occupation? and whence come you? what is your country? and of what people are you?" (Jonah 1:8). They asked their questions, took a deep breath, and there was Jonah on the spot. Now, he was disobedient, but in spite of himself he was a good preacher. So Jonah told his story, and then ended it with an extremely relevant conclusion: "I am a Hebrew; and I fear the LORD, the God of heaven, who has made"—now notice this; how relevant can you be?—"the God of heaven, who has made *the sea*"—that is the kind of God they needed, a God who had made the sea and could control it—"and [second] *the dry land*." That is where every one of them wanted to be!

This affected the mariners, for in verse 10 we read significantly, "Then were the men exceedingly afraid." Once before they were said to be afraid: "Then the mariners were afraid, and cried every man unto his god" (v. 5). In that verse they are afraid of the storm. Now they are exceedingly afraid, and the reason they are exceedingly afraid at this point is that they know something about Jonah's God.

The God of the Hebrews was not like the gods of the pagans—fickle, uncertain, weak. The God of the Hebrews was a strong God, a sovereign God. These mariners, who had visited all the ports of the Mediterranean and had heard all the port gossip, had probably heard about the Jewish God. The Jewish God was Jehovah. This was the God who had brought his people out of Egypt with a mighty hand. This was the God who had done miracles in the days of Moses and had brought death to the firstborn of Egypt. This was the God who had divided the Red Sea so the people could pass through on dry ground. This was the God who had overshadowed his people with the cloud in the days of their wandering so that they might have shade by day and heat by night. He was the God who had fed them miraculously with the manna and had given them water from a rock. This God divided the Jordan in order that they might pass over to Jericho. He made the walls of the city fall down. This God had stopped the sun and moon in the days of Joshua at Gibeon so the people would have a total victory over their enemies. This was the Jewish God. So they were exceedingly afraid. This was a very serious matter.

"What shall we do unto you, that the sea may be calm unto us?" they ask (v. 11).

Jonah answers, "Throw me overboard!"

But think of the things he could have said. He could have said, "I've told you my story; you know what the problem is. I guess we're just going to have to turn around and go back." If Jonah had said that, the storm probably would have quieted down and the boat would have had the best breeze back to Joppa that the Mediterranean had ever seen. But he did not. Instead, when he had come to this point, he had fallen so low that he said, "I would rather die than do what God wants me to do!" He did not know that a fish was waiting there to save him. He thought he was going to drown. So he said, "Take me up, and cast me forth into the sea; so shall the sea be calm unto you: for I know that for my sake this great tempest is upon you" (v. 12).

This is what happens in our disobedience. When we begin to disobey God, it is a small thing to us, not a big decision. Furthermore, God does not intervene in a great way. If you say to yourself, "I'm too tired to read the Bible this morning," or "I'll neglect my quiet time," God does not rearrange the stars of heaven to spell, "Read your Bible." He just lets you go. It is an easy decision. But a decision like that is followed by another decision in the same vein and another and another, and the way is downhill until we get so hardened in our attitudes that we say we would rather die than serve God.

The mariners were more noble than Jonah. They said, "No, we don't want to do that; we'll try a little longer. We'll row; we'll do what we can." They did their best. But the storm continued, and in the end their resolve broke down in confrontation with the harsh reality of the storm. They said, "All right, we can't do anything else. If this is what's necessary, we'll throw you overboard. Only we'll pray that God won't hold it against us." They took him and they threw him over the ship's side into the sea. The storm stopped immediately.

True Conversions

After the storm had ceased from its raging, "the men feared"—this time the word means "reverenced" or "worshiped"—"then the men reverenced the Lord." Before, they were pagans; now they are worshiping Jehovah. "Then the men feared the LORD exceedingly, and offered a sacrifice unto the LORD, and made vows" (v. 16). In other words, they all became believers at this point and were saved. They offered a sacrifice unto the Lord in keeping with the Jewish means of approach to God. "Without shedding of blood is no remission [of sins]" (Heb. 9:22). They knew that much about the Hebrew religion. So they offered a sacrifice, as if to say, "We know we are sinners; we present the innocent victim in our place." Furthermore, this was not a once-for-all action, for they promised to follow the Lord as his disciples from that time forward. That is the significance of their vows.

If verse 16 came before verse 15, I would say that this was a foxhole conversion. If we read, "Then the men feared the LORD exceedingly, and offered a sacrifice unto the LORD, and made vows; and they took up Jonah, and cast him forth into the sea: and the sea ceased from her raging," I would say that once the storm had ceased they probably all went back to being pagans again. A foxhole conversion is the conversion of a man who sees enemy troops coming up the hill and says to God, "O God, if you get me out of this, I'll do anything you want me to do; I'll even become a missionary," but who, after his life is spared, turns to his buddy and says, "Boy, we had a close call that time! The first leave we get, let's go into town; I know a place where we can really live it up!" He is saved from danger, so he is back into sin again, and he does not have another thought for God. That is what happens if the profession is before the deliverance. But in the mariners' case it was the other way around. They were delivered. Then they made sacrifices and vows.

God indicates at the beginning of the story precisely the way his sovereignty operates. Jonah said, "I'm not going to do what you want. You want me to preach to pagans, but I would rather die than preach to pagans. I'm that proud of my own religion and my people."

God said, "All right, if you're going to disobey, disobey. But it's going to be according to my rules. Moreover, I'm going to save the pagans anyway." He indicates this by saving the mariners, even though Jonah was not there to see it. God will do what God will do. But he can do it through your disobedience as well as your obedience. Happy is the Christian who learns to obey and thereby participates in the blessing.

The Second Time

There is one last point, but to see it we have to skip over to John 3:1. In my judgment, this is the most important verse in the entire book. It says, "And the word of the LORD came unto Jonah a second time."

If God had not given Jonah a second chance, we would have no cause for criticizing him whatsoever. We could only praise the name of the Lord. Suppose God had come to Jonah and had said, "Now, Jonah, I want you to understand how gracious I am. You said you were willing to have the Ninevites go to hell because you did not care enough about them to go and preach to them. You were willing to perish, but I saved you anyway. You have disgraced yourself. I cannot use a prophet who has said that he would rather die than serve me. Go home. Do the best you can. Sell insurance. But I cannot use you as a preacher." If God had said that, we could only say, "How wise our God is. Blessed be the name of the Lord!" But he does not do that. His ways are not our ways. So, in spite of all Jonah's disobedience, in spite of his sin, we read that the word of the Lord came to Jonah a *second* time.

We have to notice that the word that came to Jonah the second time was precisely the word that had come to Jonah the first time. God had not budged in his requirements. His command is repeated almost word for word; "Arise, go unto Nineveh, that great city, and preach unto it the preaching that I bid you" (v. 2). God's command had not changed, but Jonah had changed by the grace of God.

That is the way God came to Abraham. Stephen tells us in Acts 7 that God first commanded Abraham to go to a special, promised land when Abraham was in Ur of the Chaldees. So he left that city and traveled for a short time. But when he came to Haran, he settled down there. He settled down long enough for his father to grow old and die. And he was there, not in the promised land, when God came to him again, years later, with the command "Go unto a land which I am going to give you" (see Gen. 13:17). The word of the Lord came to Abraham a second time.

The same was true of Moses, whom we mentioned earlier. Moses understood that he was to be the deliverer of the people, but he took it into his mind to do it his way. He said, "The way to get rid of Egyptians is by revolution, and the way to start a revolution is by killing Egyptians." So he killed an Egyptian and had to run away across the desert to Midian. He was there forty years later when the Lord came to him, saying, "Now is the time, Moses. Now I am going to deliver the people through you." The word of the Lord came to Moses a second time.

The word of the Lord also came to Peter a second time. Peter in his brash impetuosity said, "I don't care what the others may do; I'm Peter, the rock. I won't betray you. I'll stand by you till the end." But he denied his Lord three times. Later, after his resurrection, the Lord came to Peter in Galilee in John 21 and recommissioned him. He said, "Peter, do you love me?"

Peter said, "Yes, Lord, you know that I love you."

Jesus said, "Feed my sheep." Thus, the word of the Lord came to Peter a second time.

God does that with us. He comes to us a second, third, fourth, fifth, hundredth, thousandth time. And none of us would be where we are today if God had not done that with us, because we all have most certainly disobeyed him. God is sovereign. But the sovereignty of God in our disobedience is coupled with his grace. It may be that he comes in this hour to recommission you to that to which he called you years ago. Hear him, and let your heart respond for Jesus's sake.

11

Prayer and God's Sovereignty

R.C. SPROUL

ONE OF those perennial questions that all Calvinists face from time to time and that you hear quite frequently is: If God is sovereign, then why pray? If that is the case, would not prayer be a superfluous activity, at best an exercise in meditation or some form of inspiring soliloquy? I am sure we have all had to wrestle with this question at times. Moreover, I think that it is not unlike a similar question that Calvinists also hear frequently. That is, if God is sovereign and predestination is true, why should we be involved in evangelism?

Why Pray? Why Evangelize?

In seminary I had the privilege of being in one of Dr. John Gerstner's classrooms when he was holding forth on the subject of predestination. After he had given his lecture, he began his Socratic method of discourse and started to ask us questions. That class was a seminar of about eighteen men, and we were in a semicircle. I was sitting on one end, and he started on the other end by asking that gentleman, "Now, sir, if predestination is true, why should we be involved in evangelism?"

The student looked up at Gerstner and said, "I don't know."

Gerstner went down the line to the next fellow, who said, "Beats me."

The next student said, "I always wondered about that myself, Dr. Gerstner."

Our professor kept going around the semicircle, knocking us off one by one, and I was sitting over there in the corner feeling like Socrates in one of Plato's dialogues. Plato had raised the difficult question. He had heard from all the lesser stars. Now Socrates was to give the lofty answer to the impenetrable mysteries of the question that had been raised. I was frightened. Finally Dr. Gerstner came to me. "Well, Mr. Sproul, if predestination is true, why should we be involved in evangelism?"

I slid down in the chair and prefaced my answer with all kinds of apologies, saying to him, "Well, Dr. Gerstner, I know this isn't what you're looking for, and I know that you must be seeking for some profound, intellectual response which I am not prepared to give. But just in passing, one small point that I think we ought to notice here is that God does command us to be involved in evangelism."

Dr. Gerstner laughed and said, "Yes, Mr. Sproul. God does command us to be involved in evangelism. And of course, Mr. Sproul, what could be more insignificant than the fact that the Lord of glory, the Savior of your soul, the Lord God omnipotent, has commanded you to be involved in evangelism?" I got the point in a hurry! So it is with prayer. One reason to pray is that we are commanded to pray. But in addition to being commanded to pray we are also given the privilege of prayer. Prayer for the Christian is both a duty and an unspeakable privilege.

About ten years ago, I had an experience with another theologian—Dr. Nicole—regarding this question. At that time, whenever students at Gordon College asked me questions about prayer, I would say to them, "Well, the way I do it is this: I preach like a Calvinist, but I pray like an Arminian." I said this in Dr. Nicole's presence, and I looked at him to see what he would say. He looked at me in his warm fashion and said, "Brother Sproul, I think perhaps that God would be more pleased if you would preach like a Calvinist and pray like a Calvinist as well." I did not forget that! And I thought I had better learn what it means to pray like a Calvinist.

When I began to pay attention to what Calvin had written on the question of prayer, I noticed something very unusual. As I turned to the *Institutes*, I found that Calvin prefaces his treatment of the doctrine of election and predestination (Book III, chapter 21) with a lengthy treatment of the nature and significance of prayer. I have always required that students in my courses on Calvin read Book III, chapter 20, of the *Institutes* before they even start the first chapter of Book I, so that they should be disarmed of the host of prejudices that surround the figure of John Calvin and that they might see the warmth of his heart and the passion that he had to converse in dialogue with his Creator and Lord.

Let me give a brief quotation from that chapter. Calvin writes, "But, someone will say, does God not know, even without being reminded, both in what respect we are troubled and what is expedient for us, so that it may seem in a sense superfluous that he should be stirred up by our prayers—as if he were drowsily blinking or even sleeping until he is aroused by our voice?

But they who thus reason do not observe to what end the Lord instructed his people to pray, for he ordained it not so much for his sake as for ours."[1]

So the first point in response to the question, "Does prayer change things?" is simply this: Yes, indeed prayer changes things. If nothing else, it changes us. When we come into the presence of God in conversation with him, one of the immediate benefits of that conversation is what happens to us.

The essence of prayer is adoration, confession, and thanksgiving. What happens to a person who comes daily and regularly to the throne of grace with a broken and a contrite heart? Does God's forgiveness change him? What happens to the heart that experiences gratitude and in the posture of prayer is able to recall what God has done for him? Does a grateful heart change a person? Certainly. People are changed through spending time with God.

Spiritual Treasures

But what of the thorny question concerning that kind of prayer we call supplication? What about intercession? Calvin again, in his own style, says that when we are involved in intercession and supplication we are actively involved in digging up those treasures that God has stored up for us in heaven. I like that image. The business of prayer, the prayer of supplication, is digging up those treasures that God has laid away for us. Do you remember what James said? "You have not, because you ask not" (James 4:2).

1. John Calvin, *Institutes of the Christian Religion*, ed. John T. McNeill and trans. Ford Lewis Battles (Philadelphia: The Westminster Press, 1960), 852.

Prayer Unlimited

Certainly the New Testament finds no conflict between the sovereignty of God and the effectual power of supplication for his people. But is there any sense in which God's sovereignty limits the power of prayer? Or is the power of prayer unlimited? I know that when we see answers to our prayers right before our eyes we often get very excited and sometimes overstate our position. We try to encourage everybody to pray, and we sometimes make statements like "The power of prayer is limitless! We can do anything if we just pray right!" But that is not true. In our enthusiasm and zeal for the power of prayer, we sometimes get carried away and attribute to prayer more power than it actually has. Prayer is powerful and rich. But God's sovereignty places certain limitations on our prayers.

Not too long ago a woman asked me in class, "Mr. Sproul, does prayer change God's mind?" Do you notice the difference between that question and the question we are dealing with here? It is one thing to ask, "Does prayer change things?" It is quite another thing to ask, "Does prayer change God's mind?" I looked at the woman and said, "I don't think so, if you mean by the mind of God his determinate counsel, his eternal decrees."

I would never presume to ask God to change his eternal decrees. For example, it is foolishness to think that our prayers could change the ultimate blueprint of the plan of redemption. Suppose we went before the throne of grace and said to God, "We would ask you, please, never to send Jesus back to this planet." Do you think we could change God's mind? God has decreed that his Son will return in glory, and if you pray against that from now until kingdom come, he still will come. So there are certain limitations. People have said to me, "If we really want to change the world, shouldn't we get together and pray for the conversion of Satan?" Do not waste your time! The

Word of God has made it clear that God has other plans for Satan. Besides, he does not have a mediator. So how could he be saved even if we did pray for him? These are, I hope, obvious illustrations of the way in which God's sovereignty does at least to some degree limit our prayers.

Another thing that I think we need to look at is the question of the relationship between my will and the will of God. We understand that creatures in this world are volitional beings. We have wills of our own. We have desires and requests and the ability to exercise those desires and make those requests at the throne of grace. But when we are dealing with God, we also think of God as a volitional being. We talk of our freedom, but it is limited by God's freedom. Do we think for a moment that if there is a conflict of interests between the will of God and my will, my will could possibly prevail? Certainly not! But this is the way the humanist thinks in our day, and these humanistic views often infiltrate the Christian community. A fundamental postulate of humanism is that God's sovereignty may never impinge upon or overrule human freedom. The Calvinist looks at it another way: man is free, but his freedom can never overrule God's sovereignty. Do you see the difference? It is a radical difference. It is the difference between God and no God, when it comes right down to it.

Again, we often hear Christians say, "I believe that the Holy Spirit is a gentleman and will never intrude into the life of a person without an invitation." But that is a monstrous lie! And I am glad that it is a lie, because if God the Holy Spirit had not intruded upon me, if God the Holy Spirit had not come into my heart before I ever thought of inviting him, I would not be a Christian. If God waited for us to ask him for every droplet of mercy and grace that we receive, we would be spiritually impoverished.

Again, prayer cannot manipulate God. I sometimes hear Christians saying, "If you pray like this or that or if you claim this or that, God is obliged to answer your prayer." I hear them say, "If I claim the answer to my prayer before I have any evidence that God is pleased to give it to me [I am not talking about an explicit promise in God's Word], God will grant it." I see them stand up before others in church and say, "I know that God is going to do such and such for me," and it sounds like an exercise in faith. Moreover, it sounds as if (now that they have said it publicly) God is going to get a bad reputation if he doesn't do it. But God does not have to do it.

You cannot manipulate God. You cannot manipulate him by incantations, repetition, public utterances, or your own predictions.

God is sovereign. So when you bring your requests to God he may say yes, and he may say no.

If It Be Your Will

This raises the next big question—the relationship of the will of God and the will of man. Is it proper to pray, "Not my will, but yours be done"? There are evangelicals who believe that to say "If it be your will" in the context of prayer is unbelief. But if that is unbelief, then our Lord was guilty of unbelief in the garden of Gethsemane, for he came to his Father in precisely this way. It is as simple as that. So if it is proper and fitting for our Lord to pray that way, it is certainly proper and fitting for us to pray that way.

I must add, however, there are times when we should not say, "If it be your will." There are times where God has made it abundantly clear that, if we do certain things, he will do certain things. In these cases we do not have to say, "If it be your will." He has revealed that it is his will.

Let me illustrate what I am talking about. I was out in California a few years ago, and a little old woman came up to me in a spirit of great distress. She said, "Mr. Sproul, would you please help me? I'm desperately trying to figure out the will of God for my life. Can you please help me?"

I said, "Well, what's your problem?"

She said, "I've been married to a man for over forty years, and all the time I've been married to him I've been a Christian. He's never been a Christian. He still isn't a Christian. He's been a good husband as far as the world is concerned. He's provided a living. He's been wonderful to the children. He's been faithful to me. He tolerates my religious devotion. But the things that are precious to me are not important to him, and the things that are vital to him are not important to me. I can't stand another day of this incompatibility. So two weeks ago I left my husband. Now every night he's been calling me on the phone, and he's been weeping and saying, 'Oh, Mabel, come home. I can't live without you after forty-two years.' I don't know what to do. I can't go back to him, but I can't stand his weeping and crying. Please help me find the will of God in this matter."

I said, "I'll solve your problem. The first thing to do is stop praying."

"What do you mean?"

I said, "You can stop because God has already answered your question. What does the Bible say on the question of the marriage of a believer and an unbeliever? If the unbeliever wants to depart, let him go. But if he doesn't want to depart, the believer must not depart. God's will is that you go back to your husband."

Suddenly this woman's sweet demeanor changed to outright fury. She looked at me and she said, "You wouldn't say that if you had to live with him!"

I answered, "Well, I don't know what I would say or what I wouldn't say. But, you see, you didn't ask me what I would do if I were in your situation. It's quite possible that if I had been unequally yoked to an unbeliever twenty-five, thirty, or forty years ago, I would have broken God's law long before you have. I might have bailed out in sin years ago. But you did not ask me what I would do in the frailty of my fallen nature. You asked me what the will of God is."

That woman did not want to know what the will of God is. She wanted God to change his mind. She wanted God to change his prescriptive will. She wanted God to set aside his commandment for his people and make a special case for her. And you know, she was even telling her friends that the Lord had led her to leave her husband, that she had prayed about it and felt peace. That peace did not come from God the Holy Spirit. She was praying against God's sovereignty, not within it.

I must add, however, that this woman *was* a Christian and that she eventually came to herself and went home, because she had ears to hear.

Last year I saw a television program on which a certain gentleman was being interviewed. He had become very prosperous by running a brothel which had by this time been open for something like eight years. The news commentator was asking him how he ever became involved in prostitution in the first place, and he said, "Well, I was tired of scratching about for a living, and I decided that I should try some new enterprises. I thought of opening up a brothel and hiring prostitutes to work for me. I made a covenant with God. I said, 'God, if you will bless my business for ten years, then after ten years I will give you the rest of my life in service.' And look how God has prospered me." He was serious, absolutely serious. He had asked God to bless him in his business of prostitution, and he thought God had blessed him. But he prayed against what is the clear revelation of God's Word.

I say all this in order to point out that when the biblical writers give us statements such as, "If two of you shall agree on . . . *anything* that they shall ask, it shall be done" (Matt. 18:19) or

"Seek, and you *shall* find; knock, and it *shall* be opened" (Matt. 7:7), these statements must be understood as they are qualified by other passages. We have to be careful how we deal with them.

Personal Petitions

God has invited us to come to him with our personal requests. We are to come with our supplications in a spirit of humility, as Calvin says, and yet with confidence. That is the ironic posture of prayer, the attitude of humility and boldness.

Many people come into the pastor's study and say, "Oh, please pray for me. I'm driven to despair by guilt."

"What's the problem?"

"Well, I did such and such." They then tell of a dark crime they have committed.

"Have you asked God to forgive you?"

"Yes, I've prayed for forgiveness many times, but I still feel guilty."

"Let's pray one more time."

"Why should we pray one more time? I've already prayed many times, and I still feel guilty. One more time is not going to do any good."

"Wait a minute. You've prayed for God to forgive you for that sin. This time I'm going to ask God to forgive you for something else."

"What?"

"For your arrogance."

"Arrogance? Now wait a minute. I may be guilty of stealing, murder, anger, and adultery, but I am certainly humble enough to ask God to forgive me."

"But does God say that if you confess your sins he will forgive you your sins?"

"Yes, he says that."

"Does God lie? Are you suggesting for a minute that the God of heaven and earth, in whom there is no shadow of turning whatsoever, could possibly make a promise to you that he would break and violate? Are you attributing to him the same characteristics of covenant-breaking that are so typical of you? How dare you suggest that the God of glory would break an explicit promise to his people! Let's get down and pray again, because you are determining your confidence of forgiveness on the basis of your feelings rather than on what God has said in his Word."

Do you see? People confuse forgiveness and the feeling of forgiveness, just as they confuse guilt and guilty feelings. So while we pray with humility, we also are to pray with confidence that what God has promised he will certainly do. We know that if we confess our sins, God is "faithful and just to forgive us our sins, and to cleanse us from all unrighteousness" (1 John 1:9).

God's Hidden Counsel

Finally, what about the big problem? What about the problem of what theologians call *concurrence*, the relationship between the ultimate providence of God and our human desires and activities? What about God's hidden counsel? I am not talking now about what he reveals, but about what he chooses to keep hidden. Does not Calvin say, "All events so proceed from his determinate counsel that nothing happens fortuitously"? Does not Augustine say, "In a certain sense God wills everything that takes place"? Does not Basil, that great Calvinist, say, "*Fortune* and *chance* are heathen terms, the meaning of which ought not to occupy pious minds"? Here is where the crunch comes. And that is really what this question is about. Does prayer change things? What we really want to know is the connection between what the philosophers call secondary causality and primary causality. What is the relationship?

I can answer that question, and I can answer it clearly and easily: I do not know. I have not a clue!

I used to worry about that. So I went to college and took all the courses I could take in religion. But nobody seemed to know the answer to that question. I went to seminary. I even studied under John Gerstner, and I figured that if anybody would know the answer to that question, he would. I asked him. And he said, "I don't know." I went to Europe to see Dr. Berkhouwer, and I asked him. He said, "I don't know." In fact, I have not been able to find any university that offers courses in the secret counsels of God. So when I say that "there is just one thing I do not understand," I am not pretending that I do not know only to unravel the riddle for you ten minutes later. I really do not know.

But I do know that God is sovereign. I know that he invites me to bring my petitions to him, those that are not against his prescribed will. I am invited to come into his presence, and more than that, I am even provided with a mediator who intercedes for me day and night, carrying my weak, stuttering petitions to the very presence of God. I am assisted by God's Spirit, who does know something of the secret counsels of God and who aids me in prayer. As a result, whenever I am not sure what the will of God is, I come with what the Father has given me and I leave my request with him. That is when I say, "Not my will but your will be done."

In the final analysis, that is the only answer I can give beyond what Luther said when he declared, "If God told me to eat the dung off the street, not only would I eat it, but I would know that it was good for me." That was not a stupid statement. That was a statement from a man who knew the trustworthiness of God and who was not afraid of his sovereignty. He knew that anything that God wills in the ultimate sense is redemptive, and he trusted him to that end. This was not blind trust. It was not a leap of faith. It was trust that had been acquired over a period of time in a life which had repeatedly witnessed the manifestation of God's perfect trustworthiness.

So you ask me about God's hidden counsel? I say with Luther, "Let God be God." I say with Calvin, "Wherever God has closed his holy mouth I will desist from inquiry, but where he has spoken I will speak." The Bible says that the secret things belong to the Lord our God, but that the things that he has revealed belong to us and to our seed forever.

12

Witnessing and God's Sovereignty

RALPH L. KEIPER

MY THEME is the job of witnessing in the light of God's sovereignty. But I do not merely want to give you the joys but also the theological background of witnessing and the reasons I get such joy out of giving the gospel to people. To do this I want to look at our subject in three dimensions: (1) the sinful nature of the human heart, (2) the power of the divine Word, and 3) the integrity of the believer—whether he really believes the doctrines he professes. The first of these is important in that, if we are going to witness to the world, we must understand the nature of man.

The Human Mind

Our first text is Romans 8:7–8—"The carnal mind is enmity against God: for it is not subject to the law of God, neither indeed can be. So then they that are in the flesh cannot please God."

Note the phrase "the carnal mind." This is the mind that does not have a spiritual dimension, the dimension that recognizes God.

When I was a young boy I attended the Overbrook School for the Blind. Most of us who were there were very intelligent, but our lives were built on four senses rather than five. We could hear, smell, touch, and taste. But we could not see. When anyone came into our building, we assumed that it was he who was abnormal rather than we, for we were in the majority. In fact, on one occasion, when we were having a concert, something went wrong with the electrical system and the place was in total darkness. Our visitors proved our thesis that they were abnormal, because in the darkness they could not see their way out of the building and we, who lived within our four senses, had to lead them out.

This is a situation similar to that in which we find ourselves spiritually. The world is living in a five-sense environment, but those of us who have been regenerated by the Spirit of God are living, as it were, in a six-track environment. And consequently, when we see things from a six-track point of view—which the world cannot appreciate—we can well understand that they think it is we who are abnormal rather than they.

Notice what follows from this, according to our text. The carnal mind, we are told, is "enmity against God: for it is not subject to the law of God, neither indeed can be." The reason it cannot be is that it lacks the sixth dimension. For example, if a pastor in whose church I was speaking were rather legalistic and said to me, "Keiper, there is a clock on the back wall of the church, and I want you to stop when it shows nine o'clock. And in case you do not know how to tell time, that is when the big hand is on twelve and the little hand is on nine," I might say to him, "Do not treat me as though I were an imbecile. I can tell time in English, Greek, Latin, German, or French. The numbers are all the same. I have no problem with my intellect—it is a matter of my vision. I know how to tell time; I am just not able to see the clock."

This can be applied in the following way. Many times when we witness, we endeavor to argue with people, but we would not do so if only we realized that what they need is not intelligence but vision. Moreover, we would have greater joy in witnessing if we were to realize that only the Holy Spirit in sovereign grace can provide the vision.

We have verifying data for this. In 1 Corinthians 2:14 we read, "But the natural man receives not the things of the Spirit of God: for they are foolishness unto him, neither can he know them: because they are spiritually discerned." Notice again this six-dimensional viewpoint. Or perhaps, if that is too complicated, let us make it just two tracks in this instance—just the natural man and the spiritual. The natural man is able to think, feel, will, and do many things, but because of the fall does not have that God-consciousness possessed by the Christian. Consequently, everything that smacks of revelation from God seems "moronic" to him—that is the word in Greek—it is absolute foolishness to him, for he does not have the ability to discern spiritual things.

In the tenth volume of his great work on history, Arnold Toynbee gives a very interesting illustration. He says that it is possible for a man and a dog to have great fellowship, but that fellowship must be on the dog's level, because the dog is able to communicate only on that level. He can smell us, sniff us; he can even *schleck* us (*schleck* is a sort of liquid canine greeting). But this is as far as he can go. Why? Because if a dog were to have real fellowship with men, the dog would need what we have; he would need not only a canine nature but a human nature as well. Just so, if you and I are to have fellowship with God, merely having a human nature is not sufficient, especially since we have been viciously polluted by our sinful nature. The only way we can understand divine truth is by the regenerating work of the

Holy Spirit through which we receive a divine nature and thus partake in the fullness of fellowship with God. This explains why the natural man does not receive the things of the Spirit of God, why they are foolishness to him, and why he cannot know them.

In Isaiah 55:8–9 we see that the difference between human nature and divine nature is not only a matter of degree but of kind as well. Notice the words God speaks through Isaiah: "For my thoughts are not your thoughts, neither are your ways my ways, says the LORD. For as the heavens are higher than the earth, so are my ways higher than your ways, and my thoughts than your thoughts." So there is an absolute difference between the psychology of man and the psychology of God.

There is also an absolute difference between the conduct of men and the conduct of God. In Numbers 23:19 we read: "God is not a man, that he should lie; neither the son of man, that he should repent: has he said, and shall he not do it? or has he spoken, and shall he not make it good?" Here you have the ethical contrast between man and God.

As you look at these passages and take them into consideration, you will have a clearer picture of man's mind and nature. And you need this kind of understanding in order to witness. But most important, your attitude toward the people you witness to will determine what the result will be.

Let me tell you what not to do. Years ago when I was teaching at Philadelphia College of Bible, one of our buildings happened to be at Fifteenth and Race Streets, just across from Hahnemann Hospital. Some of the doctors would come from eight to nine o'clock in the evening to render medical service to the students. I was not married at the time and lived on the property of the school. Television was just coming into existence, and the "saints" had not made up their minds whether it was proper to look at it or not. When the doctors finished their service, they would sometimes come down to my office and say, "Keiper, come on over and watch television in the doctors' lounge." I was interested in witnessing, so I went over.

Well, we would turn on the television and watch for a little while. Then we would get into a discussion, and they would turn off the set. We had marvelous sessions in theology. On one occasion one of the doctors said to me, "Ralph, I want to ask you a question. I don't want you to think I am being fresh or sarcastic, but I have a real problem. We have a number of your students working here in the hospital, and they are excellent nurses. They do their work very well. We are proud of what they do. Now, every once in a while they talk to us about being born again, and we do something we know we ought not to do. But we do it because it is fun—fun for us, at least. We give them arguments. We do not cooperate in getting born again. And I will admit that we do make them feel frustrated. But now—this is the thing that disturbs me—when they see that we will not cooperate and get born again, afterward they will have nothing to do with us socially. And my question to you is this: Do you train your students to win people to the Lord to get an A on their report card in heaven, or do you train them to be interested in the souls of men?"

I was embarrassed, as you can imagine. And yet I am glad I was asked that question, because I think it was perceptive. We evangelicals do write men off. If they will not accept the Lord Jesus Christ because we ask them, we have nothing more to do with them. This, I say to you, is the wrong attitude.

Here is another story. One Easter Monday at Columbia University in New York City, one of my professors said to me, "Ralph, will you give us an exposition of *Christ the Idiot* by Nietzsche?"

Instead of having a nervous breakdown, I said, "Give me the text." Then, just as I am giving an exposition to you now, I gave an exposition from Nietzsche. I noted that the word *idiot* comes from the Greek word *idiotes*, which can mean "unique," which Christ was. I will admit that I pulled a fast one and was a little devilish in doing it. But with joy unspeakable, spiked with glory, I proceeded.

We need to keep in mind that Calvinists should not act like Arminians when they are resisted, but ought rather to count on the sovereign grace of God. And, as I say at the seminary, "Look to him to give a zinger to the lost when they least expect it." Unbelievers can tell when we are on the defensive. They can tell when we are presenting the gospel as though we are already defeated. But on the basis of God's sovereignty we can go forth with absolute assurance, and instead of being uptight, "nasty, brutish, and short," we can with the winsomeness of grace win some for his glory.

The Divine Word

The bridge that God uses is his Word, ministered through us by the Holy Spirit. Perhaps at this point I ought to mention my frame of mind when I am preaching, teaching, or witnessing. There is a certain sense in which I can speak horizontally from my lips to the listeners' ears. This is what I do. I try to prepare my material. I try to have fellowship with the audience, to know the kind of cellophane it likes its spinach packed in. Then I deliver the message in that manner. But I have an inside secret. For I know as I preach and teach that whatever my mind and lips say—and however they say it—everything absolutely falls to the ground unless a miracle happens. So, as I stand behind the sacred desk, I lift my heart to heaven and say, "Blessed Lord Jesus, I have come to worship you in spirit and in truth. You have promised a blessing, and may your Holy Spirit do what human minds and lips can never do. Take it from here. I will be responsible for the declaration. You be responsible for the results."

I do this because, as I study the Word of God in the light of good theology, I find this was Paul's approach. If you turn to Romans 1:5, you will read, "By whom we have received grace and apostleship, for obedience to the faith among all nations, for [that is, in the interest of] his name." Paul is saying, "My business is twofold: (1) to declare and (2) to be the verifying data of what is declared, for it is the Holy Spirit's business to do the converting." When you realize that this is true, and you are spiritually and psychologically geared to this truth, you really have something going for you. It is absolutely fantastic!

Notice the great promise that God has made in Isaiah 55:10–11: "For as the rain comes down, and the snow from heaven, and returns not thither, but waters the earth, and makes it bring forth and bud, that it may give seed to the sower, and bread to the eater: so shall my word be that goes forth out of my mouth: it shall not return unto me void, but it shall accomplish that which I please, and it shall prosper in the thing whereto I sent it."

How does God do this? In Hebrews 4:12 we find a good statement of how the word operates: "For the word of God is quick [alive], and powerful, and sharper than any two-edged sword." Notice the two kinds of blades that this sword has—"piercing" (that is, the fine blade of the surgeon's scalpel) and "dividing asunder" (that is, the wide blade of the butcher's cleaver). And what is the purpose of this divine surgery? It is to discern "the thoughts and intents of the heart." If you and I really believe this, and witness knowing it is true, then we can present with authority the word which is appropriate to the person with whom we are dealing.

Let me illustrate. Sometime ago, when I was flying from Chicago to Portland, Oregon, my seatmate happened to be the public relations officer for the American Medical Association. I wondered, "How can I speak with him?" Well, first, I gave him the impression that I was a good Democrat. Medicare was going through Congress at the time. So I said, "You know, I really think you did the wrong thing in setting up the debate. I listened on NBC and CBS. You appealed to the votes you already had and not to the votes you needed." He agreed, perhaps since they had lost. I then asked, "Why are you going to Portland?"

"I am going to speak to the Oregon Medical Association on viruses." We had a marvelous time as we flew over Illinois and Nebraska, getting ill from the very viruses he was going to speak on. Finally, as we were about to fly over Colorado, he asked, "Why are *you* going to Portland?" I told him that a good friend of mine had died and that I was going to conduct the funeral service.

That brought up the interesting subject of the different ways in which one could die and how we, in particular, might like to die. We figured out all the ways in which a person can commit suicide. Then we discovered that there is one way you cannot commit suicide—crucifixion. You can get the first nail in. You can get the second nail in. If you are ambidextrous, you may even get the third one in; but you will have trouble with the fourth.

Then he said to me, "If you had the choice, how would you like to die?"

"I'm a coward," I said. "I'd like to die in my sleep."

"If you don't have your first choice, what's your second?" he asked.

"My second is to die in a plane crash."

He gulped. The stewardess asked, "Why?"

"For three reasons," I said. "One, it's fast; two, it's complete; and three, from the point of insurance, it's profitable."

"What's the matter?" the stewardess asked then.

"Nothing," I answered.

"I'm not talking to you," she said. "Your friend is getting white."

"Oh," I explained, "he forgets that this is United Airlines and that it keeps its skies friendly and gives you extra care in an emergency. What he has overlooked is not so much the idea of crashing but probably that he hasn't settled his destination."

"Is there a choice?" she asked.

I said, "There is. If we crash and are what men call dead, we will either be assured of hell or assured of heaven. For me, to be absent from the body would be to be present with the Lord." Believe me, you have a wonderful opportunity to speak about the Lord in a situation like that.

I am trying to show that sovereignty is not esoteric theology. It can be tremendous in action. But it demands that you and I must believe that the Word of God can do what it purports to do. Then we, the channels, become the means whereby the Holy Spirit takes his Holy Word and then does his work in the calling out of his elect.

The Joyful Witness

We have seen, then, that there is nothing wrong with God. And there is nothing wrong with the Word of God. So our basic problem is: If God is right and the Word is right, why do we not make a greater impact on the people about us? Approached in this way, the facts force us to admit that the fault may be ours—those of us who know the Lord are elected, born again, and eternally secure. Why do we not make the impact?

I suppose that if I talked to some outstanding surgeon, he could tell me about the science and theory of medicine and could describe various types of operations. But suppose I should ask him, "What would you say is the most important thing contributing to your success in medicine, everything else being equal?" He would say, "My skill." May I suggest that this is the point where we as witnesses fall down.

Let me show you what we need to learn before we can become skilled spiritual surgeons. First of all, we have to know our subject. This is the advice of 1 Peter 2:2–3: "As newborn babes, desire the sincere milk of the word, that you [notice the purpose clause] may grow thereby: if so be you have tasted that the Lord is gracious." One of the French translations puts it, "If so be that you have tasted that the Lord is delicious." I have no doubt that to many of us the doctrine of the sovereign grace of God is acceptable. But is it delicious? It is acceptable to our taste. But is it delicious to the point that we are willing to share it with others?

Second, we must be able to explain the doctrines. Note the admonition in 1 Peter 3:15: "But sanctify the Lord God in your hearts: and be ready always to give an answer [an 'apology' or 'defense,' not a retort]." I have an idea that when a good doctor is consulted, the reason he is consulted is that others assume first that he knows his subject and second that he can explain it. This is what God expects of us. We are not to give a retort. We are not to be on the defensive. We are not to be uptight. We are to be sold out to the Lord and so steeped in the knowledge of his Word that we are able to give a reason to every man that asks us. And we are to do this in meekness and with respect. Even to the sinner, God would have us be gracious. We are to be the picture book to lead him to the written Book that he might come to see the Living Book, even Jesus Christ our Lord.

Now I want you to see a play on words. Notice 1 Peter 3:15: "But sanctify the Lord God in your hearts: and be *ready* always." Look at that word *ready*. It means "to be prepared," and that means that we must give time to our task and plan for it. I am positive that most of us have no problem at that point. But now look at Romans 1:15: "So, as much as in me is, I am *ready* to preach the gospel to you that are at Rome also." The word *ready* in Romans 1:15 is another word, in this case the "ready" of having no mental reservations whatsoever. It is what Paul is expressing when he writes to young Timothy: "I know whom I have believed, and am persuaded that he is able to keep that which I have committed unto him against that day" (2 Tim. 1:12).

Here is my personal testimony. I have been to Moody Bible Institute, Lafayette College, Eastern Baptist Seminary, and various universities. So for years I was ready to witness in the sense of 1 Peter 3:15. But I was not ready in the sense of Romans 1:15. How did I get ready? Well, there was a time when I needed an eye operation. Dr. Fry was the eye surgeon at the University of Pennsylvania Hospital, and for eight years he tried to get me to have it. He told me that the ratio of success was one thousand to one. But I said to him, "What if I am that one? Moreover, it's my eye, not yours. I'm emotionally connected to it. Don't argue with me intellectually. I know my emotional problem. Let's forget it." So he forgot it. A doctor cannot do a thing unless you are willing to cooperate.

Then one night I did a very stupid thing. I was preaching in Philadelphia, and I chose a subject which I should not have chosen. I chose "The Sufficiency of God's Grace." Well, I was preaching along when all of a sudden the Holy Spirit did a discourteous thing. He said to me, "Why are you lying to these people? You know that God's grace isn't sufficient. It's not sufficient for you. It hasn't been for eight years."

I said, "Holy Spirit, don't ruin a good sermon. Why can't you tell me tomorrow? Let's argue it out then. If you keep this up, you're going to confuse me."

He said, "Since I am sovereign, I will keep this up."

Well, I began to speak faster; I began to speak louder; I began to speak with great intensity; I think I even pounded the pulpit. But the more I tried to speak, the louder the Holy

Spirit became. Then he made the decisive move. He brought to my mind the thought that "perfect love casts out fear" (1 John 4:18). Perfect love! Mature love! Then he said, "You have the fear; what about the love? Do you think that if you totally lost your vision, God would not be able to take care of you?"

I said, "Lord, I want to see. I am not interested in your care at this moment."

He said, "I realize that, but let's settle it tonight. I am sovereign. You're the slave."

I said, "Lord, you're confusing my mind; you're causing tension. You're going to ruin my sermon."

He said, "I'll tell you what to do—let's ruin it. Let's be charitable tonight and give the people two sermons for the price of one."

Well, I stopped preaching what I was preaching and told the congregation what the Holy Spirit was telling me. The next morning, I called Dr. Fry and said, "I am willing to have the operation."

He said, "Would you come to my office and give me a psychological record of what caused you to change your mind? I have many, many patients who have the same problem, and I don't know how to handle it. Their problem is not intellectual. It's fear."

I said, "Dr. Fry, frankly, it is not a psychological problem. It was downright raw unbelief. I did not take God at his word."

If God is sovereign, he is going to have us serve him on his terms, not ours. And it may be that he is going to confront us with things which we love more than him. God in his sovereign grace is going to haunt us. He is going to be "the hound of heaven." God in his sovereign grace loves us so much that he is going to be on our trail until we allow him to conquer. But when he does, when we surrender and say, "Not my will but yours," then the joy begins to come and, instead of being the victim of a problem, we become more than conquerors through him who loves us.

13

Optimism and God's Sovereignty

ROGER R. NICOLE

AN OPTIMIST does not cut a very impressive figure among Christians. There are too many bad things around us—how can anyone be optimistic when faced with our world situation? There is the threatening of evil on varied horizons. The church is despised. There are people who are turned off on Christianity altogether and who think of Christians only with contempt and sometimes verbalize that contempt. In the presence of the quasi-collapse of our very civilization, how can we be optimists? When there are so few signs of redeeming value on the horizon, how can we possibly expect that somehow things will turn out for the best?

There are people who like to contrast optimism not only with pessimism but with realism. They say that if you have an understanding of what is really going on, you cannot be an optimist. And yet, Romans 8:28–39, written (I think we would be glad to recognize) in circumstances and times hardly more promising than those in which we live, contains an expression by Paul of the most far-reaching optimism: "All things work together for good to them that love God" (v. 28). We do not have to fear anything, he says. There is no problem which can defy the power of God to solve it.

The climax of this optimistic passage is the great statement that *nothing* "shall be able to separate us from the love of God, which is in Christ Jesus our Lord" (Rom. 8:39). Separation is the great source of human sorrow. The places where separations occur—the airport now, previously the wharf or railroad station—are often places of tears because people who love each other are separated there, at least for a while. The cemetery is a place of tears because it separates us for this life from those we have loved. One of the great concerns we have is that somehow we cannot stay with the things and people we love. We cannot take them with us.

Separation, therefore, represents a most formidable threat to human life. It is the constant threat of disruption in the middle of the quietness and peace of our lives. So the Christian naturally may raise the question, "Can the blessings that I have found in Jesus Christ be taken away from me? Does separation threaten this as well? Could it be that after I have for a while found the loving arms of the Savior I may be ripped away from his embrace and lost forever?" It is in answer to these questions that the apostle speaks to us. He says, "I am persuaded, I am absolutely convinced, I am positive." It is difficult to translate this exactly in English. "I am persuaded" refers to a completed act which issues into a present attitude. It means, "I am completely sure and positive that nothing can separate us from the love of God manifested in Christ Jesus, our Savior."

King of Fears

In listing those items that cannot separate us from the love of God, Paul begins with the most formidable threat—death. Surely death is the key representative of separators. It separates those who die from their labors, belongings, and activities. It separates them from the fulfillment of their careers. It separates those who remain from their fellowship, company, and presence. Moreover, it is a separation which has a tone of finality that other separations do not have. We may be sent to a concentration camp, but there is always a hope that somehow we might come back. But when death has spoken there is no return. In that sense, death is the king of fears; it is the emperor of separators.

This is where Paul starts. He starts at the highest pitch, as it were, saying, "Death cannot separate us from the love of God manifested in Jesus Christ." Here we must think of the situation of the apostles when the Lord died. They thought that death had separated them from him and him from them. They were confused and bewildered. They were distraught. They were using the verb *hope* in the past, saying that they "had hoped" (Luke 24:21 NIV), meaning that they did not hope anymore. They were grieved about their own weakness in his last moments and uncertain about their future. It seemed that lightning had struck in the middle of the highest experience of their lives and that it had broken down and dispersed everything they held dear. But it did not separate them from the love of God in Christ Jesus.

In fact, Christ's death is the principle of salvation and union that he came to accomplish. The apostles did not understand it then, but later on they learned that the death of Christ was the seal of his love for them and the basis of their acceptance with God. Far from being a separation between them and God, Christ's death was actually a great bridge of union. In it the words of the Lord in John 12:24 (NIV) became literally true—"Unless a kernel of wheat falls to the ground and dies, it remains only a single seed." It cannot bear fruit. "But if it dies," then it bears much fruit. In the death and resurrection of Christ, the disciples were to see and understand this great and eternal unity that was secured and established by God between himself and his people.

The question arises: Granted that the death of Christ did not separate, what will happen at our death? Will *our* death separate? Will death produce a barrier between Christ and us, as it does between human beings? What is behind this dark barrier that marks the passage from one life to the other?

The Scripture teaches that our death in no wise separates us from Jesus Christ. Paul, in the epistle to the Philippians, says that he was in a quandary as to what he should prefer—to continue his labor on the earth or to die. To die would be far better, he says, because then he would be with Jesus Christ. Our death, then, is not to be seen as a catastrophe that writes a final period after a life of many weaknesses and vacillations. On the contrary, it is a climactic bridge that leads us into a firmer and fuller fellowship with God than anything we have known in the days of our flesh. Beyond the doors of death, the Christian can see the Lord of glory waiting and welcoming him to his presence and to the joy of heavenly fellowship. Even as Stephen, filled with the Holy Spirit, could look beyond the doors of death and martyrdom to see the Son of Man rising from his seat at the right hand of God, so too can we see the welcoming gestures of the Savior, who, having died for us, is prepared to receive us into the place that he has prepared for us.

We should not have mournful Christian funerals. It is true, of course, that the Christian, even more than the non-Christian, senses the loss of someone he has loved. But the time when a Christian passes from this scene into eternity is a time in which we ought to sing, "Hallelujah, for the Lord God omnipotent reigneth." Here is one whom God has redeemed, one who has come to the fulfillment of his time on earth, and death has not separated him from but rather united him with the Lord.

How true, therefore, that death cannot separate us. Death more properly can be seen as uniting us. The death of Christ unites us with him. Our death, more than anything we have experienced heretofore, brings us into a full fellowship with him.

Worse Than Death

Now we must examine the second term in Romans 8:38: Paul is persuaded that *life* shall not separate us. At first this seems puzzling. What does Paul mean? Life is not really a separator. Life unites; life is the time in which we can establish and consummate unions. Life is a time in which fellowships can be initiated and enjoyed. Why should life be considered a threat? Was Paul just stringing words together loosely without wanting to emphasize anything in particular? Was he just taking these things in pairs—death and life, angels and demons, height and depth—without attempting to relate them to anything in particular? I doubt that very much, for life also often separates. In fact, there are separations in life that are even more painful than death.

There are people, for instance, who vow faithfulness to each other in marriage. They say, "We will always be together and always love each other. Forsaking all others we will cherish each other only." Unfortunately, not so far removed from the church is the divorce court, in which people confess that their vows meant nothing. They confess that their love has crumbled to pieces and that they are so incompatible that it is a burden and pain for them to live with one another. They ask the state to dissolve the union. Is not death, in a sense, almost preferable to this?

There are parents who are terribly disappointed in their children. In the days of their youth, these children are the objects of their parents' affection and care and sometimes loving discipline, but somehow they grow estranged from the family and in some cases dishonor a name distinguished by years of dedication and service. There are parents who are so grieved about what their child is doing that some of them may be heard to say, "I wish he had died when he was a baby. He only brings grief to me in my old age."

Moreover, there are Christians who ask this question: Will my life separate me from the love of God manifested in Jesus Christ? Is it possible that after I have been the object of his loving care and after I have turned to him in response to the invitation of his grace, I may so persist in my iniquity, so harming myself in my unbelief, so dishonoring his name, that God will say, "I am sick and tired of you; I don't want you in my heaven. You are not worthy to be received in the everlasting courts"? Is it possible that our resolve may be so weak and our willingness to obey the Lord so frail that somehow in spite of all the blessings that God has bestowed upon us we may still turn away from him and move back into our own wickedness? Does this not threaten us? Is there not something here that we need to fear, something that must qualify our assurance and joy as we bask in the sense of the presence of God and his blessings? I think it is in answer to this kind of query, brought with trembling heart and voice, that the apostle speaks to us in these inspired words: "I am persuaded, that . . . life . . . shall [not] be able to separate us from the love of God, which is in Jesus Christ our Lord" (Rom. 8:38–39).

We are here reassured, not in terms of our own stability and firmness of resolve, but rather in terms of the wondrous perseverance of God, who in his grace will not abandon those in whom he has begun his good work. He will pursue constantly and repeatedly the work of his grace to lead us safely at last into the kingdom of his love.

Voice from Hell

People argue that, if that is so, then surely the Christian can go ahead and indulge the wickedness of his own heart. He can wallow in debauchery, feel free to despise and exploit his fellow men, be a racist, chauvinist, sexist, and whatever else you can mention—and he need not fret about it. He can cultivate ambition and materialism, pride and selfishness. He can make his phone a network of gossip. He can lie, cheat, rob, falsify. Indeed, he can do anything he pleases, and nothing will happen to him. There are people who think that the doctrines of grace are almost like the traffic of indulgences that existed in the days of Luther, when people seemed to think that by buying indulgences they could secure a license for sinning without bearing sin's evil effects.

When this argument arises, I ask, "Do you merely want to develop a theological discussion, or do you really mean that? Do you really mean to use this argument as the rule of your own life? If you really mean this, if you really mean to say that if you only had assurance that you could escape the evil consequences of your sin, you would readily associate yourself with evil and sin, whatever might be the effect of that upon the heart of God, then what makes you think that you are saved at all? What makes you think that this kind of attitude reflects the regenerating power of the Holy Spirit?" I do not want to be unduly harsh, but I must say as God's servant that this is not the voice of heaven. It is the voice of hell. If you want to sin without having the consequences of it, then your heart has not yet been renewed by the Holy Spirit.

Do not entertain the idea that perseverance exists to encourage sinners in sin. That could never be the case. In the words of the apostle Paul, "God forbid; never; let it not happen!" Never, never in your life can you say, "Let us sin, that grace may abound." That is completely wrong.

Our Faithful God

But there is another case. Maybe you do not want to sin but you are well aware of your weakness. You say, "I know myself only too well. I have experienced many forms of God's grace, but I am still inclined to go astray, to go to the right and to the left, and to fall into the terrible abyss of my own depravity. I cannot say whether or not I can cling to the Lord. I know that the grasp of my hand is too weak even to hold to the rope of salvation he has extended to me. I lament over it. I am afraid of myself." This person knows the awful significance of the warning of Scripture that says, "Let him who thinks he stands take heed lest he fall" (1 Cor. 10:12). He is also aware of the warning that it is impossible to renew again to repentance those who once having tasted the good Word of God have fallen away.

What assurance can we give to this person? We can point him to the words of our text: "I am absolutely positive that life will not separate us from the love of God manifested in Christ Jesus." It is not because you are so persevering, for you are not. It is because God is persevering. It is not that you are so strong and that your grip is solid; it is that he is faithful and his grace marvelous. As you sense your own weakness, I encourage you to look to the Good Shepherd. Look at his feet and see there the mark of the nails. Look at his side and see there the mark of the spear. Look at his hands and see there the mark of his love for you. Then hear his voice which says, "I love my sheep. I give my life for them. I give them eternal life; they shall never perish, and *no one* can take them out of my hand."

14

The Sovereign God and the Church

JOHN R. W. STOTT

THE PURPOSE of our sovereign God is not just to save isolated individuals, but to call out a people for himself. Moreover, his purpose is to make this people what by his eternal intention and decree they already are, namely, a holy people, a people distinct and different from every other people, in fact, a new society for the new age that dawned when Jesus came. That is what we are. It is a sweet dream, a fragrant ideal, a beautiful vision—this new society for the new age—until you turn to the concrete, ugly realities of the contemporary church.

Once in a church in Scotland, somebody had been doodling during the sermon. I suppose the sermon had been a bit boring, so a member of the congregation had started drawing pictures of the preacher and then writing verses. When the service was over, the janitor found this little poem:

To dwell above with saints in love,
Aye, that will be glory.
To dwell below with saints I know,
Now that's a different story.

That is the difference between the ideal and the reality, the sweet dreams that we have of a new society for the new age and the concrete realities of the Christian church today. Despite the signs of church renewal, there is a long way to go. So my theme is the Lord and his church, and I propose that we look back to the very beginnings of the church on the day of Pentecost as described in Acts 2:42–47.

As we compare the twentieth-century church with the first-century church, it is important that we face the realities of both. There is a tendency among some Christians to idealize the early church, to romanticize the church of the first century. We look back wistfully through rose-tinted spectacles and speak of it as if it had no blemishes. This is not right. The early church had hypocrisies and heresies just as the church does today. Nevertheless, one thing is certain: the early church for all its failures was nevertheless deeply stirred by the Holy Spirit. The Holy Spirit had come upon the church, shaken it, and filled it so that the church had begun to be the temple of the living God, the very place in which the living God dwelt in the midst of his people.

So the question we are going to grapple with is: What are the marks of a Spirit-filled community? What evidences were there of the presence and power of the Holy Spirit in those early days? What evidence did that early church give that it was the church of the sovereign Lord Jesus Christ? What are the marks of the Holy Spirit's activity that we should expect to see today?

Apostolic Teaching

The first mark of the Spirit-filled community is instruction or study, for the very first thing we are told about this early community is that "they continued steadfastly in the apostles' doctrine" (Acts 2:42). This newly constituted body of Christ was a learning and studying church. In it the Holy Spirit moved God's people to study and submit to God's Word. Is that not remarkable? Is that the first mark you would have chosen if you had been describing a Spirit-filled Christian community? I think very few people would have chosen that, but that is what Luke puts first. They devoted themselves to the apostles' teaching.

Note that they were not reveling in some mystical experience that led them to despise their intellect, disdain theology and doctrine, or suppose that instruction was superfluous. Nor did they imagine that just because the Holy Spirit had come to the church he was the only teacher they needed and that they should therefore dispense with human teachers. No, they devoted themselves to the teaching of the apostles. And in so doing, they submitted to the authority of those whom Christ had called, chosen, and authorized to be the teachers of his church.

As they submitted to the teaching authority of the apostles, that authority was authenticated to them by miracles, as we are told in verse 43—"Fear came upon every soul: and many wonders and signs were done by the apostles." The very apostles to whose teaching authority they submitted were those whose authority was authenticated by their ability to work miracles. That is why we call the book of Acts "the Acts of the Apostles." All but two of the miracles in the book of Acts were performed by the apostles. And the only two exceptions were by people on whose heads the apostles had laid their hands, authorizing them to take part in a particular apostolic ministry.

We are not limiting miracles to the apostles. We believe God is free and sovereign and therefore able to perform miracles today. But if we are to have a biblical doctrine of miracles, then we must agree with the apostle Paul in 2 Corinthians 12:12 when he says, "The signs of an apostle were wrought among you in all patience, in signs, and wonders, and mighty deeds." The major purpose of these miracles was to authenticate the infallible teaching authority of the apostles. So these early Christians submitted to that authority as it was mediated to them.

What does that mean for us today? Well, today the doctrine of the apostles is to be found in the New Testament. The major reason we accept this precious Book is that it is the teaching of the apostles. The criterion by which the early church in the third and fourth centuries decided which books were to be admitted into the canon of the New Testament was: Were they written by the apostles or, if not, did they come from the circle of the apostles with their imprimatur? The test of canonicity was apostolicity. So the New Testament is the teaching of the apostles, those infallible teachers whom Jesus Christ called and authorized and filled with his Holy Spirit; it is in the New Testament that the doctrine of the apostles in its definitive form has come down to the church of every place and age. A church that is filled, led, and ruled by the Spirit will always submit to this authority.

A Spirit-filled church is a biblical church. I thank God that in my own Anglican communion, when the bishops gathered for the Lambeth Conference in 1958 and spoke of the unique authority of the apostles as witnesses to Jesus Christ, they drafted this sentence: "To that apostolic authority the church must ever bow." The church is not over the Bible. The church is under the Bible. So the church must bow to its authority.

What is true of churches is true also of individuals. One of the clearest evidences of a Spirit-filled Christian is a hunger for Scripture, a humble submissiveness to the authority of Scripture as God's written Word. Show me a Christian who loves to meditate on the Word of God in private, believes that it is God's written Word, is eager to join a Bible-study group in which to study it with other Christians, delights to come to church on Sunday for the public exposition of the Word of God by a pastor authorized to do so, and seeks to conform his or her thinking and living in every particular to the Word of God, and you are showing me a Spirit-filled Christian. But show me a Christian who is not devoting himself to the apostles' teaching, who neglects his Bible, disregards it, who is not adorning the truth with a holy life, and you show me one who may not have received the Holy Spirit at all, let alone have been filled with him.

The first mark of the fullness of the Spirit is that we devote ourselves to the apostles' teaching. That is why theology is so important. The Holy Spirit leads us as a church to take this seriously, which is not surprising, because the Spirit is the Spirit of truth. Wherever the Holy Spirit is in power, truth is honored. Wherever the Holy Spirit is reigning, truth reigns with him.

Fellowship and Generosity

The second mark of a Spirit-filled community is its fellowship, for we read that the early Christians continued not only in the teaching of the apostles but also in fellowship. The word *fellowship* was born on the day of Pentecost. There was no fellowship before then, no true fellowship. The word for fellowship is *koinonia*, and it refers primarily to our participation in God: Father, Son, and Holy Spirit. Thus, John writes at the beginning of his first letter, "Our fellowship is with the Father, and with his Son Jesus Christ" (1 John 1:3). Paul adds to this when he speaks of the "fellowship of the Holy Spirit" (2 Cor. 13:14 NIV). We have that common participation in God. It is what makes us one.

But *koinonia* does not only bear witness to what we share *in* together. It also bears witness to what we share *out* together. That is why the Greek word for *generous* is *koinonikos*, a related term. *Fellowship* refers not just to what we participate in together—our common share in Father, Son, and Holy Spirit—but to our giving as well. For this reason Luke goes on immediately to speak of sharing, showing how these early Christians shared their lives and goods with one another. In Acts 2:44 we read that all who believed "were together" (I do not think this means they all lived together, that the first Christian commune was established in Jerusalem, but only that they loved each other and wanted to be together) and "had all things common." The word for *common* is *koina*, which is also related to the word *koinonia*. One of the ways in which *koinonia* can be exhibited is through a sharing of goods. They even, so we read in verse 45, "sold their possessions and goods, and parted them to all men, as every man had need."

Let us think carefully about this. Does it mean that every Spirit-filled Christian community will follow suit literally? Does it mean that every Christian who is filled with the Holy Spirit will convert his assets to cash and give the cash away? I think our first answer to that must be yes, at least in some cases. Some people have done this down the centuries of the Christian era, and I myself do not doubt that the Lord Jesus still calls a minority of his followers to a life of voluntary and absolute poverty. I believe that there are some, like the rich young ruler, whom Jesus calls to give away everything and to follow him in poverty—in order, no doubt, to witness to the rest of us in the church and world that a man's life does not consist in the abundance of his possessions.

But having said that, we have to add, if we are balanced Christians, that neither the book of Acts nor any other part of the New Testament justifies the view that private property is forbidden to Christians and that every Christian should therefore give it all away. It is interesting that in this very context, in Acts 2:46, we read that they broke bread "in their homes" (NIV). So evidently at least some of them still had homes. They had not all sold them.

The sin of Ananias and Sapphira was not that they were stingy or that they kept back part of the sale of their goods. It was that they kept back a part while pretending to give the whole. Their sin was hypocrisy, not miserliness. So the apostle Peter distinctly says in that confrontation that it was entirely within their discretion whether they would sell their property or not, and having done so, it was theirs to determine what proportion they would give away. "While it remained," Peter said to Ananias, "was it not your own? and after it was sold, was it not in your own power?" (Acts 5:4). In other words, every Christian has to make his own responsible decision before God concerning the level at which he is going to live, how simple his lifestyle is going to be, how much he gives away, and how much he keeps for himself. There is no rule that we can lay down for everybody. Each one must make this decision conscientiously before God.

But I am not going to let you (or myself) off the hook quite as easily as that. For we must realize that many of these early Christians, although they were not obliged to sell their property—it was their own—nevertheless they did give their goods away. What I learn from this is that these earnest, Spirit-filled Christians were generous Christians. They shared what they had with people in need. They could not live in affluence when other people were in need.

Generosity has always been a mark of Spirit-filled Christians, because God is a generous God. Do you know what "sovereign grace" means? It means sovereign generosity. That is what grace is: generosity. So every Christian who is submitted to the sovereign will of our sovereign God undoubtedly will be generous also.

The fundamental principle is plain: they distributed to all "as every man had need." This principle has come to be distilled in the socialist creed "from every man according to his ability and to every man according to his need." I know that the very word *socialism* sends some people up the wall, but I dare say that this is a principle to which every Christian should subscribe whatever his political allegiance. Is it not a biblical principle? From every man according to his ability, to every man according to his need. Of course, how you work it out politically and in economic terms is another question. I am not giving a political sermon. But I am preaching the Bible, and the biblical faith does have strong political implications. Our responsibility is to accept that where there is human need, there we must show Christian compassion.

Thank God for this early Spirit-filled community. These Christians were filled with compassion, and therefore they loved and cared for one another. Christian fellowship is Christian caring, and Christian caring is Christian sharing. The first fruit of the Spirit is love. So where the Spirit is, there is love; and where there is love, there is also generosity, and not least in our own world in which the needy nations and the underdeveloped parts of the world beg at our gates like Lazarus. Is their need on our conscience? It will be, if we are filled with the Spirit.

Formal and Informal Worship

The third mark of the Holy Spirit is worship, for we read that they "continued steadfastly in the apostles' doctrine and fellowship, and in breaking of bread, and in prayers" (Acts 2:42). In Greek the definite article is found before each of the expressions—*the* breaking of *the* bread and *the* prayers—so they seem to refer primarily to the Lord's Supper, on the one hand, and to prayer services rather than to private prayer, on the other. In other words, since they were filled with the Holy Spirit, these Christians loved to meet one another not just for fellowship and instruction, but for worship as well.

Notice this about the balance of the early church's worship. To begin with, it was both formal and informal, for it took place both in the temple and in private homes (Acts 2:46). It is notable that the early Christians continued to worship in the temple for a while. They did not immediately abandon the institutional church, as many do today. No, they worked, I have no doubt, to reform it from within according to the gospel. I am positive that they did not attend the sacrifices of the temple, because they had come to understand that these sacrifices had been fulfilled by the sacrifice of Jesus. But they did attend the prayer services of the temple. And they supplemented these services with their own more informal meetings in each other's homes. Young people, impatient with the inherited structures of the church, could well learn a lesson from these early Spirit-filled Christians. For the way of the Holy Spirit with the institutional church is more the way of patient biblical reform than of impatient rejection.

I am saddened by the contemporary polarization of the formal and the informal. Some people love to come to church for a dignified service. Others like to get out their guitars and meet in each other's homes. Why polarize? Why choose? Can we not have them both? I believe that every healthy church should have the more dignified, reverent, and formal structured service *and* a place where we can get out our guitars and sing and clap each other on the back—if we want to do that kind of thing. Hug one another. Let your hair down, if you have any and are exuberant. Why not? Why cannot we have both formal and informal, like the early Christians?

Not only did they have the formal and the informal, but their worship was joyful and reverent. There is no doubt of their joy. The Greek word in verse 46 means "exaltation." The New English Bible calls it "unaffected joy." There was joy in those early Christian worship services because they had something to celebrate. They believed in the mighty acts of God in Jesus Christ. They believed in the sovereignty of God in salvation, revelation, creation, and judgment. We could learn from that. Some services, even in Reformed churches, are too lugubrious. There is not enough joy. Oh, dignity is permissible. What is unforgivable in Christian worship is dullness. For how can you be dull when you are worshiping God and have something to celebrate? Christian worship is celebration. That is why I thank God for trumpets and singers and drums and strings, so that we bring not only our voices but also our instruments to celebrate the praises of God.

A Salvation Army drummer was once hitting his drum so hard that the organist begged him to be a bit quieter. But the drummer said, "God bless you, sir, since I've been converted I'm so happy I could bust the bloomin' drum!" Then, if I may turn to the opposite end of the ecclesiastical spectrum, Geoffrey Fisher, Archbishop of Canterbury, said, shortly before he died, "The longer I live the more convinced I am that Christianity is one long shout of joy." Not bad for an archbishop!

But notice, it is very significant that alongside that joy is fear. For we read in Acts 2:43, "Fear came upon every soul." *Fear* means reverence. This tells me that although the early Christians were joyful, their joy was never irreverent. They knew that God was in their midst, and they bowed down before him in awe and wonder. It is a mistake to imagine that whenever the Holy Spirit is present in power there is nothing but noise, shouting, clapping, timbrels, and dancing. Sometimes when the Holy Spirit is present in power there is great quietness and even silence as people bow down and worship. Joy *and* reverence! Formality *and* informality! Dignity *and* exuberance! These go together.

Biblical Evangelism

The fourth mark is evangelism. The last verse (Acts 2:47) says that "the Lord added to the church daily such as should be saved." Notice this about their evangelism. First, the Lord did it. The sovereign Lord added to their number those who were being saved. I have no doubt that his sovereignty in salvation was expressed through their witness, preaching, and example, but the Lord did it. In these man-centered days, is it not important that we get back to the God-centeredness of biblical evangelism? The Lord Jesus adds people to the church, and nobody but he can do it.

Second, the Lord did two things at the same time: he saved people and he added them to the church. He did not add them to the church without saving them, and he did not save them without adding them to the church. He did the two together.

Third, he did it every day, for there were daily conversions. The early church did not say, "Let's organize a church mission every five years. Once every five years we'll have an evangelistic effort, and then we'll sink back into our respectable bourgeois mediocrity for the rest of the time." No, it was every day! Day by day there was outreach into the community, for they loved people who were not yet saved and prayed that the Lord would add them to the church.

The conclusion is this. As we look back over these four marks of a Spirit-filled community, we notice that they all concern relationships. Those early Christians were related, first, to the apostles. They were eager to receive the apostles' instruction and so were an apostolic church anxious to maintain and practice what Christ and his apostles taught. Second, they were related to each other. They continued in the fellowship. They cared deeply about one another because they were one in the Spirit. Third, they were related to God. They worshiped God both at the temple and in their own homes, in the Lord's Supper and in the prayers, with joy and with reverence. A Spirit-filled church is a worshiping church. And fourth, they were related to the world outside, for they were engaged in continuous evangelism. No self-centered, self-contained church can claim to be filled with the Holy Spirit, for the Holy Spirit is a missionary Spirit, and a Spirit-filled church is a missionary church.

These four marks are exactly what young people are looking for all over the world. There are multitudes of young people who are voting with their feet, leaving the churches today, because they are disenchanted even with the evangelical establishment. Why? What are they looking for? They are looking for a ministry that is biblical, in which the apostles' teaching is related to the contemporary world. They are looking for a warm, loving, caring fellowship. They are looking for worship that is real, because God is in the midst. And they are looking for outreach, a compassionate outreach into the needy world.

The day of Pentecost has come, and it will never come again. The Holy Spirit came in power, and he has never left the church. He is here. But what we need is to submit afresh to this sovereign Spirit. We need to allow him the lordship that is his over the body of Christ. We need to seek the liberating power of this sovereign Spirit. Then, when the Spirit again dominates and rules the church, there will again be the apostolic doctrine, a loving and caring fellowship, joyful worship, and an ongoing, outgoing evangelism.

15

Soli Deo Gloria

ROGER R. NICOLE

A GOOD portion of what follows is not original with me. I have derived a great deal of assistance from a very remarkable address entitled "The Sovereignty of God." It was given at a meeting of evangelical Christians in 1929 by a man who was for many years dean of an evangelical seminary in southern France—Emile Doumergue. The latter half of this chapter is virtually a free translation of a portion of that address.[1]

An Epitaph

The words of this Latin title are well known. They are a veritable motto of the Reformation, and they mean, "To God alone be the glory." *Soli Deo* means "to God alone"; *Gloria*,

1. A similar address, based on Doumergue, was published in the October 23, 1964 issue of *Christianity Today* under the title "Divine Sovereignty: Cornerstone of the Reformation."

"the glory." The Reformation people were very eager to express themselves with that word *solus*. They talked about the Bible alone—*sola Scriptura*. They talked about faith alone—*sola fide*. They talked about grace alone—*sola gratia*. And then they said, "To God alone be the glory"—*Soli Deo Gloria*.

In a very remarkable way, these words could stand as an epitaph for one of the great leaders of Reformed thought, John Calvin. Calvin has no epitaph because he has no tomb. He had directed that when he died his body should be taken in a simple box of pine wood and be buried in Plainpalais Cemetery without ceremony and without any marker. In some cases the people of Geneva were not eager to follow his leadership. They gave him plenty of trouble during his life. But after his death they managed to fulfill at least this request. So the place where Calvin is buried is unknown, and as a result, there is no epitaph for him.

I would like to suggest that *Soli Deo Gloria* would be a suitable epitaph for him because that idea was veritably the master spring of his life. Here was a man who was concerned not to gain anything for himself—in money, fame, influence, affection, friends, or any other way. He was concerned only that the name of God be exalted, that God's glory shine out in the city of Geneva, which he had come to love so greatly, and beyond the walls of Geneva into the devastated lands of his native France.

To this end Calvin labored prodigiously throughout the days of his life. He did not allow himself to be stopped by sickness. When he died at age fifty-five, he was suffering from gout, rheumatism, an ulcer, colic, and recurrent headaches. But this man, in spite of poor health, problems in his family, and the hatred and maneuvers of enemies who were often not at all particular about the methods they used—this man continued to write, serve, preach (sometimes six times a week and twice on Sunday), discuss cases, deliberate, govern, organize, and prepare the people of Geneva to magnify the Word of God. So it is, I think, proper to affix this epitaph to his life: "To God alone be the glory." Here was a man who was concerned to assert, develop, and exemplify in his life the sovereignty of God.

An Inescapable Doctrine

There are people who say, "If you talk about the sovereignty of God, you are in danger." There is the danger that one may begin to talk about predestination. There is the danger that one may begin to talk about radical corruption. There is the danger that one may begin to talk about the definite purpose of God in the death of Christ for those whom he planned to redeem. There is the danger that we may speak about judgment and resurrection. And all those things are not very palatable nowadays. "Let us talk about things that are more suitable," we are told. "Let us talk about things that are more accessible, more winsome, so that our generation may be won." But the Scripture does not seem to be concerned about these objections. I fully grant that we ought, whenever possible, to be winsome. There are no dividends in being more "ornery" than we need to be. But our desire to be winsome gives us no right to modify or soft-pedal any element of the truth God has delivered.

When you examine Scripture, it is quite obvious that the Bible presents God as sovereign. And this is the great truth that the Reformers—not only the people of the Reformed Churches (Zwingli, Calvin, Farel, Beza, and others) but Lutherans as well, and the Reformers of England—were very ready to acknowledge and emphasize.

When they said that God is sovereign, they recognized that he is sovereign in the distribution of the knowledge of himself, in the impartation of his truth. The sovereignty of God leads to the recognition of an inspired Bible that is authoritative from cover to cover. It is not a mixture of errors and truths so that we have to go through the painful task of discerning the truth and rejecting the error. It is the Word of God, which alone is able to give us guidance, which alone is able to provide for us the light that we need, which is the norm by which everything else must be judged and which no other norm can judge. Therefore the Reformers emphasized the authority of Scripture, and they rejected, on one side, anything in the Roman Catholic tradition that tended to undermine or minimize the impact of this authority and, on the other side, the approaches of the enthusiasts and free seekers who thought they could take their pick from the Bible, keeping what they liked and rejecting what they did not like.

When you talk about the sovereignty of God, you also talk about the supreme excellence of the triune God whose perfections are made apparent throughout the Scriptures, in nature, and particularly in the plan of redemption. Whoever speaks about the sovereignty of God must speak about God's justice, his holiness, his consummate love, his eternity, his immensity, and about all the other dimensions of this prodigious being that we can begin to understand only when we yield our minds to the revelation of the Scripture.

The sovereignty of God has an impact upon our view of man. On one hand, it lends dignity to man, for men and women are created in the image of God. Every member of the human race is the bearer of the image of the sovereign God, and because of that each is invested with infinite value far beyond anything that our material society can provide. On the other hand, recognition of the sovereignty of God implies that as his creatures we are obliged to conform to his commandments, that we cannot set forth for ourselves a system of ethics, rules, and style of life that suit our fancy, that we are commanded to live under the sovereign command and authority of God himself.

When this is recognized, it is immediately apparent that God's standards are so high that none of us can possibly hope in any way to meet them. Thus, the sovereignty of God immediately crushes man as sinner into the very dust of the ground, for he is unable to rise in God's presence but must be the object of his condemnation.

When we speak about the sovereignty of God, we speak about God as sovereign in the plan of redemption. Jesus is not some man who merely hoped to be acceptable to God, not somebody who (like other men or even more than other men) had a consciousness of the divine. Jesus Christ is God himself, God the Son coming down to our earth to share in our situation, take upon himself the burden of our sins, and bring us redemption. No one but God himself could work that out for us. God in Christ bore the awful burden of our penalty in its fullness in order that we might be liberated from the terrible guilt of our sins before the judgment bar of God, so that we might be redeemed, washed, and justified in the presence of God and rejoice in the blessings that he has provided for those who belong to him.

When we talk about the sovereignty of God, we emphasize the sovereignty of God the Holy Spirit, who works in the lives of men, not awaiting consent from unregenerate sinners but transforming lives that are disrupted, distorted, and destroyed by sin. He plants within the very heart of sinful man the principle of a new life and reorganizes, reorients, reforms, and renews in every possible way that which sin has damaged or demolished. This Holy Spirit in his gracious mercy does not only originate new life, but he develops, nurtures, seals, and preserves it for the final day of fulfillment. Even at death he completes his work in the soul, and at the time of the resurrection he perfects the work in glory for the redeemed, who are then fully renewed in the image of Jesus Christ.

When we speak about the sovereignty of God, we speak of his sovereignty in the life of the church. God's people do not have simply a society or organization of their own devising, but they are gathered together under the guidance and leadership of God himself, speaking his Word and moving by his Spirit. We speak of God working through sacraments, the sacraments that he himself has established and instituted, whose number has been determined by him, and whose form has been communicated to us. Their efficacy is controlled by him. Their administration must be in accordance with his Word. Their blessing is enjoyed when there is an obedient acceptance and reception of that which he himself has prepared.

When we speak of the doctrine of the sovereignty of God, we recognize that he will be sovereign at the last day. This is a sovereignty that has its beginnings in eternity past, that carries through the long and checkered history of mankind and that will not abate at the last. For at the last day, the Lord Jesus Christ himself will appear. At the last day, the power and the glory of God will be made manifest. Then he will sit on the throne of judgment to manifest his glorious love in the redemption of those whom he has redeemed, and his glorious justice in the condemnation of those who are rightly condemned for their sins.

There is no place in theology where the sovereignty of God has no impact. There is no place in theology where we can say, "Here I can forget about it, and I can move along other lines." The sovereignty of God is like a ray of light that permeates the totality of the theological enterprise.

Immorality Checked

But then objections arise. Some argue, "All this sounds good (or perhaps does not sound so good), but is it really possible?

Can we really hold any view like that? If we say that God is sovereign, what will happen to morality? If we say that man cannot under any circumstances produce good works, then are there really any ultimate differences between actions? Does that not wipe out from the very start the whole principle of distinction between good and evil among men? Does that not make morality impossible?"

I suppose one could proceed to discuss this in a theological manner—to examine arguments, consider objections, and line up points in an orderly disposition. I would like, however, instead of going into a theological discussion, to challenge you in terms of a historical consideration. In the Reformation, there was a group of men who made precisely these assertions. Over against the prevailing current, they said that man is radically corrupt and is therefore totally unable by himself to please God. He is incapable of gathering any merits, let alone merit for others.

But did these assertions damage morality? Were these people a group of scoundrels who satisfied their own sinful cravings under the pretense of giving glory to God? One does not need to be very versed in church history to know that this was not so. There were at that time thefts, sexual sins, dishonesty in the sphere of government and politics, murders, unjust wars. Even within the church there was a heinous and shameful trafficking of sacred positions. But what happened? These people, who believed that man is corrupt and that only God can help him, came forward like a breath of fresh air. They brought in a new recognition of the rights of God and of his claim upon the lives of men. They brought in new chastity, new honesty, new unselfishness, new humbleness, and a new concern for others. "Honest like the Huguenots," they used to say. In some cases, when tempted to free themselves from great difficulties by lying, they would not perjure themselves but instead stuck to the truth even to the death. Immorality was not promoted; it was checked by the recognition of the sovereignty of God.

“That is impossible,” some say. Yet it happened.

True Freedom

Others say, “If we assert that God is sovereign, freedom will be impossible. Man will lose his power of making choices and his sense of responsibility before God. If God has decided everything, man is reduced to the level of a puppet or a robot.” I do not know if there is anything so fearfully bad about puppets and robots. I suppose in their place they have their value. But surely all of us would agree that this is not the role which God has provided for men; and so, if men and women are reduced to puppets and robots, then we have made a serious departure from the biblical representation of man.

But again, rather than going into the arguments of the matter, let us merely examine what happened in the sixteenth century when the sovereignty of God was asserted. Did the people involved allow themselves to be robbed of all initiative? Were they reduced to slavery under the power of God? Not at all! On the contrary, they were very keenly aware of their responsibility. They had the sense that for everything they were doing, saying, and thinking, they were accountable to God. They lived their lives in the presence of God, and in the process they were pioneers in establishing and safeguarding precious liberties—liberty of speech, religion, and expression—all of which are at the foundation of the liberties we cherish in the democratic world. Far from eclipsing their sense of freedom, the true proclamation of the sovereignty of God moved them toward the recognition and expression of all kinds of human freedoms which God has himself provided for those whom he has created and redeemed.

"It is impossible that this should happen," we are told. Perhaps! Yet it happened!

Vigorous Activity

People also say, "If you teach the doctrine of the sovereignty of God—that God directs and appoints everything, 'decreeing whatsoever comes to pass,' as the Westminster divines were led to express it—this will ruin the whole value of human activity. There is no point of exerting yourself in any way." From this perspective recognition of the sovereign superintendence of God seems to be in conflict with the significance and value of human activity.

But again, we may make an appeal to history. What did these people—Calvin, Farel, Knox, Luther—what did they do? Were they people who reclined on a soft couch, saying, "If God is pleased to do something in Geneva, let him do it. I will not get in his way"? Or, "If God wants to have some theses nailed to the door of the chapel of Wittenberg Castle, let him take the hammer. I will not interfere"? You know very well that this is not so. These were not people lax in activity. They did not abdicate their responsibilities as God's instruments. They were not lazy. Calvin may be accused of many things, but one thing he has seldom been accused of is laziness. No, when the sovereignty of God is recognized, meaningfulness comes to human activity. Then, instead of seeing our efforts as the puny movements of insignificant people unable to resist the enormous momentum of a universe so much larger than ourselves, we see our activity in the perspective of a sovereign plan in which even small and insignificant details may be very important. Far from undermining activity, the doctrine of the sovereignty of God has been a strong incentive for labor, devotion, evangelism, and missions.

"Impossible!" Yet it happened.

God's Men, God's Women

In the first century, the world was in a frightful condition. One does not need to be a great authority on Roman history to know that. There were signs of the breakdown of the Roman Empire—rampant hedonism and a dissolution of morals. But at that point God was pleased to send into the world that great preacher of the sovereignty of God, the apostle Paul, and this introduced a brand-new principle into the total structure. The preaching of Paul did not avert the collapse of the Roman Empire, but it postponed it. Moreover, it permitted the creation of a body of believers that persisted through the terrible invasions of the barbarian hordes and even through the Dark Ages.

At the end of the fourth and the beginning of the fifth centuries, the threat was perhaps even more serious, for now paganism had crept *into* the church. Pelagianism reasserted the claims of man—man capable, sufficient, able to help himself, from whom God could not require anything more than he was able to accomplish. But at that point God raised for the defense of the truth that great servant of his, that great preacher of grace, Augustine of Hippo, one of the most influential men between the apostle Paul's day and the present time. Here again the appearance of Augustine did not dispel all clouds; it did not avert all the shipwrecks of individuals or even of churches; but in the presence of the monstrous threats of humanism, even within the church, it safeguarded the truth of the gospel centered in the grace of God and his sovereignty.

In the sixteenth century, once again the church had succumbed to deep corruption. It was corrupt "in its head and members." In many ways it was a cesspool of iniquity. People did not know how to remedy the situation. They tried councils, internal purges, monastic orders. None of these things seemed to work. But God again raised up to his glory men who proclaimed the truth of his sovereignty, the truth of God's grace. In proclaiming this truth, they brought a multitude of the children of God into a new sense of their dependence upon and relationship to Christ. In proclaiming this truth, they benefited even the very people who opposed them in the tradition of the church. They are small, these men of the Reformation. They had little money, little power, and little influence. One was a portly little monk in Germany. Another was a frail little professor in Geneva. A third was a ruddy but lowly little man in Scotland. What could they do? In themselves, nothing. But by the power of God they shook the world.

Radically corrupted but sovereignly purified!

Radically enslaved but sovereignly emancipated!

Radically unable but sovereignly empowered!

These men were the blessing of God for our world.

Today we face a similar situation. Today also there are everywhere the signs of disillusionment and of collapse. There are threatening clouds on the horizon. There are threats without and within. There is a frightful degradation of morals and lowering of life. May God raise up men and women who believe in the sovereignty of God and who proclaim it and live it! The world needs them now!

What Is the Alliance?

The Alliance of Confessing Evangelicals is a coalition of believers who hold to the historic creeds and confessions of the Reformed faith and proclaim biblical doctrine in order to foster a Reformed awakening in today's church. Our members join to share the gospel, engage the culture, and equip the church for the glory of God. We serve the church through broadcasting, events, and publishing.

The work started in broadcasting and continues with *The Bible Study Hour* featuring James Boice, *Mortification of Spin* with cohosts Todd Pruitt and Carl Trueman, *Theology on the Go* with Jonathan Master and James Dolezal, *Every Last Word* featuring Philip Ryken, and *Dr. Barnhouse & the Bible* with Donald Barnhouse. Alliance broadcasts acquaint millions worldwide with the life-changing message of the gospel through radio, the internet, apps, and podcasts.

Our events include the Philadelphia Conference on Reformed Theology, the oldest, continual, national Reformed conference in North America, and regional events, including theology and Bible conferences. Pastors' events, such as Reformation Societies, continue to encourage, embolden, and equip church leaders to pursue reformation in the church.

Place for Truth is our online magazine—a free "go-to" theological resource. *reformation21* provides cultural and church critique. Our online daily devotionals include *Think and Act Biblically* from Dr. Boice and MatthewHenry.org, a resource fostering biblical prayer.

Alliance publishing also includes books from a list of trustworthy authors, including titles such as *Entering God's Rest, Knowing the Trinity, Our Creed,* as well as a vast list of affordable booklets and e-books such as *The Authority of Scripture* and *How to Pray.*

The Alliance further seeks to encourage sound, biblical doctrine by offering the most extensive English library of Reformed biblical and theology audio in the world at ReformedResources.org.

For more on the Alliance, visit AllianceNet.org.